History of the
THEATRE

History of the
THEATRE

ROBIN MAY

WHSMITH
EXCLUSIVE
·BOOKS·

For Maureen

Photographic acknowledgments

BBC Hulton Picture Library, London, 243; Bridgeman Art Library, London, 52–53, 76/Somerset Maugham Collection 88, 90–91/Mander & Mitchenson Theatre Collection 156–157/Private Collection 160/Victoria and Albert Museum 106, 111; Donald Cooper, London, 10–11, 14–15, 73, 75, 84–85, 92–93 top, 93 bottom, 102, 136, 141, 182–183, 200, 201, 202–203, 204, 208, 213 top and bottom, 215, 216–217, 219, 220, 222, 223, 224–225 top, 226, 227, 229, 230, 232, 233, 234–235, 239, 242 top, 244–245, 246; Deutches Theater-Museum, Munich, 96–97 bottom; Dominic Photography, London/Zoë Dominic, 58, 60, 61, 72, 86–87, 112 top, 125, 137, 146, 162 top, 168–169, 173, 184, 192–193, 199, 207, 210, 218, 221, 224 bottom, 231, 237, 238, 240–241, 242 bottom, 252/ Catherine Ashmore, 82, 109, 112 bottom; Frank Driggs Collection, New York, 181 top, 185; Dulwich Picture Gallery, London, by permission of the Governor 42, 46; E.T. Archive, London, 20–21, 78, 152–153/Garrick Club, London, 94/Peter Joslin Collection 114; Mary Evans Picture Library, London, 6, 7, 13, 23 bottom, 26, 30, 33 top, 39, 44, 80, 81, 96 top, 101, 103, 104, 107, 108, 110 bottom, 115, 120, 122, 123, 132, 145, 148, 149, 151, 155, 158, 159; Fred Fehl, New York, 181 bottom, 190 bottom, 194 top and bottom, 196, 197, 198 top and bottom, 205; Giraudon, Paris, 66–67, 68, 69, 74, 77/Lauros-Giraudon 32, 79; Robert Harding Picture Library, London, 24, 25; Japanese Information Bureau, London, 26–27, 28 bottom, 29 bottom; Kobal Collection, London, 171, 180; Longleat House, Wiltshire, by permission of The Marquess of Bath, 47; Manchester City Art Galleries, 121; Mander and Mitchenson Theatre Collection, London, 95 bottom, 105, 126, 131 bottom, 144 top, 147, 162, 166, 172/Angus McBean 135, 140, 176–177, 191; Mansell Collection, London, 8 top, 16, 17, 28–29 top, 31 top and bottom, 33 bottom, 34 left, 34–35 bottom, 35 top, 45, 51, 62, 70 left, 70–71 top, 98–99, 116, 202; MAS, Barcelona 63, 64, 65; Robin May, London, 43, 86, 113, 164 top/Peter Cotes 178/Zoë Dominic 214/Houston Rogers Collection 170/Angus McBean 236/Trustees and guardians of Shakespeare's birthplace 54; National Portrait Gallery, London, 41, 59, 83/Tate Gallery, London, 118; Peter Newark's Historical Pictures, Bath, 57, 95 top, 100, 119, 124, 127, 128–129, 130, 131 top, 133, 142 bottom, 154, 164 bottom, 182, 189, 190 top, 195; Novosti Press Agency, London, 138 bottom, 138–139 top; Photoresources, Canterbury, 8–9 bottom, 9 top; Picturepoint, London, 12; Popperfoto, London, 206; Press Association, London, 228; Royal Academy of Art, London/Private Collection, 89; Royal Shakespeare Company, London, 55; Scala, Florence, 18–19 bottom, 19 top, 22, 23 top, 36–37, 38; Martha Swope Associates, New York/Martha Swope, 247, 248–249, 251/Carol Rosegg 250; John Vickers Archive, London, 14, 48, 49, 110 top, 117, 134, 142–143 top, 144 bottom, 163, 165, 167, 174, 175, 179, 186–187, 188, 211, 212

Front cover:
The School for Scandal at the Theatre Royal Haymarket, London in 1983. Left to right: Patrick Godfrey, Beryl Reid, Sebastian Shaw and Dulcie Gray.
Back cover:
Paul Schofield as Prospero and Nicky Guadagni as Miranda in *The Tempest*, 1975.
Title spread:
Bernard Shaw's *Heartbreak House*, 1983.
Left to right: Rosemary Harris, Diana Rigg, Charles Lloyd Pack, Mel Martin, Rex Harrison and Paxton Whitehead. (Dominic Photography, London. Photos Zoë Dominic)

This edition produced exclusively for
W H Smith

Published by
The Hamlyn Publishing Group Limited
London · New York · Sydney · Toronto
Bridge House, Twickenham, Middlesex TW1 3SB, England

Copyright © The Hamlyn Publishing Group Limited 1986
ISBN 0 603 03896 4

Printed and bound by Graficromo s.a., Cordoba, Spain

CONTENTS

The
ANCIENT WORLD

All theatre springs from the same ultimate and universal source, the religious dances of primitive peoples. They are still performed in parts of the world and are dances of thanksgiving, dances to exorcize evil spirits, prayers, war dances and so on. The legends of a tribe could be acted out in dance and in song, so theatre in its very widest sense goes back to the dawn of humanity.

Ancient Egypt

Though Western drama springs from Ancient Greece, the Egyptians were revelling in lively religious plays more than 2,000 years earlier. A play from 3,200 BC found at Luxor, the ancient Thebes, in 1895 concerns the creation of the world by Betah, god of Memphis, and into it was inserted the Isis-Osiris-Horus legend, with Set, god of Evil, murdering

Osiris, god of Good and of Life. Later in the proceedings Osiris is resurrected and the world is put to rights again.

Egyptian temple dramas were by no means elitist. The gods were treated as familiar friends and everyone knew their stories. The best staged and costumed plays appear to have taken place at Abydos and Busiris. Professional actors played the leading parts, pilgrims the minor ones, while the audience shouted and laughed. The whole entertainment seems to have been a triumph for players and public alike, though, for a religious drama, very rowdy.

Descriptions of actors, plays and audiences that have survived show how important the theatre was to the Egyptians. Despite their apparent pre-occupation with death, what we know of their theatre suggests a healthy appetite for life. Though plays were mostly staged

Right: Horus is suckled by Isis in the papyrus swamp.

Opposite: All theatre springs from the religious dances of primitive man. This is a harvest dance in Papua, New Guinea.

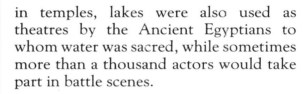

Far left top: The actors and chorus of a satyr play portrayed on a vase. They are carrying masks. Note Hercules with his club on the top row.

Left: Actors holding their masks make an offering to Dionysus. From Piraeus, Greece, c.400 BC.

Far left bottom: The magnificent theatre at Epidaurus in Greece, which dates from the fourth century BC.

in temples, lakes were also used as theatres by the Ancient Egyptians to whom water was sacred, while sometimes more than a thousand actors would take part in battle scenes.

Greece

Greek drama grew out of the dithyramb, which was a hymn chanted to humour the god Dionysus, god of fertility and wine, whose cult reached Greece from the Near East. We have Aristotle's word for this, though some have challenged it, and also dispute that Greek comedy sprang from phallic songs.

The dithyramb was sung by a 50-strong male chorus, which portrayed half-human, half-animal satyrs, complete with phallus. It is said that lyrics were introduced to the dithyramb in about 600 BC by the poet and musician Arion of Methyman.

A century later Thespis appeared on the scene, a poet and the original Thespian, the name frequently given to actors in the past. Dryden wrote of 'Thespis, the first professor of our Art, At country wakes sang ballads from a cart'. It was Thespis who introduced an actor to talk to the chorus and its leader. He won the first prize at the original dramatic contest in 534 BC. An annual contest was instituted by Pisistratus, Tyrant of Athens, with awards for writing and acting dithyrambs and tragedies. As for Thespis's famous cart, it was his way of transporting his troupe about, and it also served as a stage.

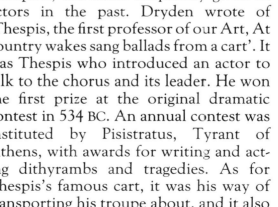

Overleaf: A scene from Peter Hall's 1981 production of the Oresteia at the National Theatre, designed by Jocelyn Herbert.

It was from these simple beginnings that the glorious age of Greek drama began, an age that was to last until about 300 BC. The influence of the Greek style of theatre lasts to this day. Even the most unhistorically minded visitor to the great Greek Theatre at Epidaurus could hardly fail to note its kinship with the Olivier auditorium in Britain's National Theatre. Two great annual festivals were held in Athens: the City Dionysia every spring for four days, featuring mostly tragedies, and the Lenaea every January for three days, which was a festival of comedy. Satyr plays were written by the tragedian in addition to his three plays for the Dionysia. They were grotesque and obscene farces burlesquing the tragedies. A day at the City Dionysia therefore consisted of three tragedies and a satyr. The cost was considerable, so a government official not only chose the lucky participators but found wealthy patrons for the dramatists.

The theatre of Dionysus, marvellously sited below the Acropolis, was used for the festivals. In early years the spectators sat on wooden seats and audiences included slaves, and women, who sat in the upper part of the amphitheatre. Clapping denoted approval, whistles and stamping the opposite. Everyone had a metal token with his or her seat number on it; everyone was allowed to comment on the proceedings. The first theatre of Dionysus has vanished, except for a few stones, but the site remains the same. Today's theatre dates from 330 BC and the stage area from AD 61.

In 525 BC the founder of European drama, Aeschylus, was born. He was the author of the Oresteia and of 89 other plays, four of which survive. Aeschylus introduced a second actor into plays, making true drama possible, as distinct from an actor conversing with the chorus. He also gave the theatre painted backdrops and basic properties. Except in *The Suppliants* he cut the chorus from 50 to 12. He encouraged fine costumes and introduced the cothurnus, or high boot, which with the onkos – a huge headdress – made figures most imposing. The tragic actor wore a mask of linen, wood or cork,

Below: Performances are given each year at Epidaurus (seen here) and at the Theatre of Dionysus in Athens.

Left: The masks worn by Greek actors – there were no actresses – bore the essential features of the character they were playing and were made to help the voice carry.

of which there were more than 30 types. The mask was made to assist voice projection in the huge theatres.

As a dramatic poet Aeschylus ranks second only to Shakespeare. His range must have been colossal judging by what survives of his works, his language monumental. His trilogy about the family of Agamemnon – the doomed house of Atreus – and their crimes against the gods ranges awesomely wide, a saga of vengeance, sin, suffering and, inevitably,

divine justice. They can be enjoyed by even those who know nothing of the traditions of Greece and its drama. The other surviving plays are *The Suppliant Women*, *The Persians*, *Seven against Thebes* and *Prometheus Bound*. *The Persians* takes place at the palace of the defeated King Darius of Persia, not in Athens. The playwright had fought against the Persians at Marathon, Salamis and Platea.

The work of Sophocles (496–406 BC) is mainly lost to us, only seven of his tragedies, part of a satyr play and a few fragments surviving. He defeated Aeschylus at a Dionysia when he was 27 and won 18 prizes in 30 years. He added a third actor, then a fourth, providing plays that are more complex than Aeschylus's, more intimate and full of human feeling.

No Greek dramatist appeals more to modern taste and no Greek play is better known than *Oedipus Rex* (also known as *Oedipus Tyrannus*), with its six speaking parts, two of which are as famous as any in Shakespeare – Oedipus and his mother Jocasta. This masterpiece finds Sophocles excelling in the individual hero's tragedy, in relationships with the gods and fate; and his heroes suffer for a sin regardless of innocence or intention. (The most famous modern Oedipus has been Laurence Olivier with the Old Vic at the New Theatre in 1945, his mother being played by Sybil Thorndike. Those who saw this epic performance try vainly to describe the great cry that Olivier uttered when Oedipus hears the terrible truth – that he is the son and murderer of Laius,

Below: Laurence Olivier as Oedipus in the Old Vic production of Oedipus Rex *at the New Theatre in 1945. This legendary performance was later seen in Paris and New York. The director was Michel St. Denis.*

the son and husband of Jocasta. It must surely haunt the rafters of the theatre still.)

Sophocles also wrote *Oedipus at Colonus* in which the aged Oedipus is redeemed by suffering. Others have tried, but none have matched the *Oedipus* of Sophocles.

Eighteen of Euripides's plays survive of more than 90 that he wrote. Born in

484 BC, this questing intellectual humanist brought a realism to the theatre that startled his contemporaries, even though he used mythical characters. He won only five prizes, perhaps because he presented human emotions, not universal dramas of principle. He attacked vendettas and even war, as in *The Trojan Women*. Women are the leading characters in many of his later plays (although they were played by men). He wrote a number of tragi-comedies, notably *Iphegenia in Tauris*, which had a happy ending. *Medea* treats the themes of a mixed marriage and infanticide, *Electra*, infanticide. Other plays include *Helen*, *Orestes*, *Hecuba*, *Iphegenia in Aulis* and *The Suppliant Women*. His surviving masterpiece is *The Bacchae*, produced the year after his death, which is an ecstatic,

Above: The Greeks, staged by the Royal Shakespeare Company, featured 10 plays centred on the Oresteia *legend, produced and adapted by John Barton. John Shrapnel, Mike Gwilym and Lyn Dearth are pictured.*

elemental, explosive play. The puritanical King Pentheus is contrasted with Dionysus – Bacchus, god of joyousness, wine and fertility. There is a famous scene where the King, disguised as a woman, watches the Bacchantes in a frenzy whipped up by Dionysus. Later Greek dramatists and the Roman Seneca were influenced by him, and his popularity remains strong.

The last of the great quartet of Greek playwrights was Aristophanes (448–380 BC). Eleven of his 40 comedies survive complete. Nine are 'old comedy', with the chorus playing a major role in the action. Forty-two years before the playwright was born comedy had been admitted to the Dionysia, and the great comic satirist, with no censorship worries, used it to promote the cause of freedom. He wrote loosely connected scenes and his plots were often fantastic and political, mocking people and institutions. His 24-strong chorus wore masks and padding that exaggerated the stomach and rump, and sometimes a phallus. His best known play is *Lysistrata*, in which the Greek women deny their husbands sexual intercourse until the long war between Sparta and Athens is ended. *The Birds* has two Athenians opting out of city life and heading for an ideal state, which leads them to the kingdom of the birds, who, they suggest, should form a utopia.

People start queueing up to join them in their state half way between heaven and earth. Widely regarded as his masterpiece despite the fact that now obscure topical allusions abound – it would seem to be a satire on Athens – it is written in matchless comic poetry.

Actors in Greece were well treated: they had their own union, the Artists of Dionysus were excused military service, and could safely travel abroad to perform. The chorus, poets, coaches and musicians were likewise privileged.

An essential feature of Greek drama was the Aristotelian play. The philosopher Aristotle (384–322) analysed tragedy in his *Poetics* and comedy in a book that is lost. He tried to analyse the tragic drama of Euripides' and Sophocles' plays, especially the former's *Oedipus Rex*. He demanded a coherent start, middle and finish, stirring content to move an audience to fear and pity and therefore be purged of their emotions: catharsis. He did not in fact demand obedience to the unities – of time, place and action – although Renaissance writers claimed that he did. He claimed only unity of action, though he devised a 24-hour time span. Brecht and others have challenged Aristotle, but much great drama, and not just famous French plays, has been influenced by him, including many Elizabethan tragedies and Ibsen's *Ghosts*.

Rome

Roman theatre was so inferior to Greek, so blood-drenched at its worst, that the popular image of it, immortalized by Hollywood, of gladiatorial combats, mass slaughter of people and animals, and thrilling chariot races, is by no means inaccurate. However, it did have some very important features.

Roman drama was derived from the Greek version, usually with no chorus, and with comedy far more popular than tragedy. Its time span is roughly from 300 BC to AD 500. The famous games held every September date back to the rule of the Tarquins in the sixth century BC. Chariot racing was always a huge attraction. In about 300 BC farces and dialect plays were added to the games, the genre stemming from Campania. The gladiators first trooped out to death or glory in 264 BC. The crowd took to the 'sport' at once, but at least they were watching trained professionals. This bloody addition started in the year that the First Punic War with Carthage broke out, with prisoners making up the gladiatorial ranks. The war ended in 241, and the following year plays became part of the entertainment, for which Livius Andronicus (not to be confused with his more famous namesake Livy) provided translated Greek plays.

Roman comic drama was doubtless patronized by many of those who revelled in the arena. Rome's two finest comic writers were influenced by the Greek Menander (c.342–c.292 BC). By reputation he was master of the 'new comedy', comedy of manners with stock characters and the chorus providing occasional musical relief. His plays can perhaps be claimed as the ancestors of modern comedy and they influenced Plautus and Terence greatly. Menander's work was unknown in modern times until four incomplete plays of his were found in 1905. One of them, *Periciromene*, was complete enough, however, to allow the scholar Gilbert Murray to turn it into *The Rape of the Locks* (1941). There have been two other finds, establishing that he was a

Left: On this vase painting an old miser is being threatened by thieves as he hangs on to his treasure chest, c.350 BC.

master of sophisticated social comedies, with the chorus kept to a minimum.

Of the work of Caecilius, regarded by some as finer than Terence or Plautus, only some 300 lines survive.

Plautus (c.254–184 BC) was originally an actor, perhaps a clown. He was certainly a master of farce, as well as of comedy and stagecraft. Twenty-one of his plays survive. He was a great exploiter of mistaken identities, disguises and so on. His plays are full of family figures, cunning slaves, vainglorious warriors and courtesans, and are sometimes set in brothels. Broader than Terence, he remains funny today. Several of his plays were woven into the musical *A Funny Thing Happened on the Way to the Forum*. He influenced Renaissance dramatists including Shakespeare (*The Comedy of Errors*), Molière and Ben Jonson.

Terence (c.190–159 BC) was a Carthaginian slave who was educated by his Roman master. His six known plays are better made and subtler than Plautus's and have fewer traditional characters. His servants are bunglers rather than rogues. In *Andria* a young gentleman falls in love with a young woman of his own class, which was not a feature of Greek comedy, as young women were kept in seclusion in Athens. Criticized for adapting Greek originals, he was not as popular as Plautus, partly because the public was developing a preference for gladiatorial combats and circuses. He, too, influenced Renaissance writers, notably Molière.

There is no surviving Roman drama written for the stage, as the nine tragedies of Seneca (c.4 BC–AD 65) were written to be read. This is just as well, perhaps, for some of the scenes are hardly stageable, including one where a grieving father puts together his son's disembered body. Nor are the plays constructed in a truly dramatic manner. The horrors and sensations taken from Greek legends and, perhaps, life in Nero's Rome, are paraded rather crudely as far as characterizations are concerned. If they were ever staged it must have been in stylized form. They include *Medea*, *Phaedra*, *Agammemnon* and *Hercules Furens*, and influenced Renaissance writers, notably of the Revenge tragedies of Elizabethan England, including *Titus Andronicus*, and the masterpiece of the grisly genre, *Richard III*.

The first Roman theatres had to be made of wood by Senatorial decree. The Senate ordered a stone one to be pulled down in 154 BC, apparently considering a permanent stone building devoted to plays an affront to public morality. However, by 55 BC Pompey was ordering a stone one to be built. There are remains of Roman theatres still to be seen, with

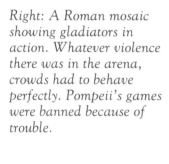

Right: A Roman mosaic showing gladiators in action. Whatever violence there was in the arena, crowds had to behave perfectly. Pompeii's games were banned because of trouble.

Left: Actors preparing for a performance.

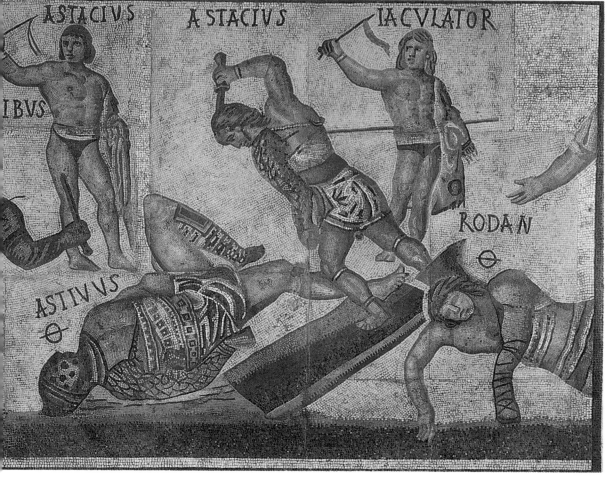

ASTACIVS   ASTACIVS   IACVLATOR

...IBVS

RODAN

ASTIVS

Overleaf: The Roman theatre at Orange in France, dating from c.AD2. The skene, or stage building, in front of which Greek actors performed had now given way to a much grander edifice.

19

fine examples at Aspendus and Orange.

The Romans built on level ground rather than on hillsides, encircling the auditorium with a wall, which was sometimes decorated. The orchestra was halved to a semi-circle, and the skene covering the whole diameter of the stage raised. The wall at the back of the stage was decorated with doors and openings, and in later theatres a curtain which was lifted upwards rather than dropped was introduced. To counter the heat awnings could be drawn over the auditorium, and the atmosphere was cooled by slaves sparkling rosewater into the air.

The religious festivities from which the Greek theatre sprang had no part in the Roman theatre. Most of the actors were slaves trained by a manager. For all their lowly status they could become very famous: Roscius, who died in 62 BC, was the most famous comic actor of his day and was earning a fortune in his prime. He lives on as a synonym for a great actor, including a mention by Polonius in *Hamlet*. The great nineteenth-century black actor, Ira Aldridge was known as the American Roscius.

Roman costumes were modelled on Greek ones. Height was increased by buskins, masks and wigs were worn and costume colours had significance. Old men wore white, young ones purple, courtesans yellow and parasitic characters grey. Hair colour was also significant, with white for age, black for youth and red for a slave.

Roman comedy gradually degenerated. The *mimus* was knockabout farce with a stock of crudely drawn characters. It was

Below: This detail of a wall painting is at Herculaneum. It shows a tragic actor after a performance. Note his mask.

Below: Ancestors of folk like these entertained in the Dark Ages.

very bawdy and – for the first time – had women taking part. The *pantomimus* was cruder still, with correspondingly coarse singing and dancing.

With the growth of Christianity all forms of theatre came under attack, and in the sixth century Justinian ordered them all to be closed. The Church in the Byzantium element of the Roman Empire also reacted against the theatre, closing all theatres there in the seventh century.

The Dark Ages

The so-called Dark Ages enveloped Europe and the theatre is often said to have gone underground at this period, which symbolically it did. What theatre there was went back to basics. It survived through wandering minstrels and actors who gave performances in courts and halls, market places and fairs. These custodians of theatrical tradition had many names: mimi, jongleurs, histriones and so on, and they sang, danced, mimed, made music and performed acrobatics. Their stages were open spaces and raised platforms, and they ranged the whole of Europe. Yet it was to be the Church, not these indomitable entertainers, which would bring the theatre back to true life again.

ORIENTAL THEATRE

India

A form of theatre appeared in India in the first century AD, at about the time it was languishing in Europe. It was essentially religious, performed in temples and palaces. The stages set up inside the buildings were consecrated before performances. They took the form of complex dances with symbolic gestures and were about the lives of the gods and of royalty. This form reached its peak between the third and eighth centuries, when it started to decline. The actors were wandering professionals, with stages erected for each performance. Not until 1776 was there a permanent theatre in India, built by the British in Calcutta.

Classical Indian drama was written in Sanskrit, some historical, some mythological, some about more ordinary folk. The earliest known plays were written by Bhasa in southern India. There are 13 of them, some legendary stories from the Sanskrit epics such as the *Mahabharata* and the *Ramayana*, but also a play now well known outside India, *The Little Clay Cart*, with characters who would be familiar to a Roman audience, including a clown and a half-witted prince.

The most famous Indian (Sanskrit) dramatist is Kalidasa, born in the late fourth century. Three of his plays survive, the romantic comedy *Malavika and Agnimitra*, *Vikrama and Urvashi*, in which a mortal marries a nymph and has fights in heaven, and *Shakuntala*, in which a king marries a hermit's daughter. Western readers have noted a resemblance to Shakespeare's late romances, notably *Cymbeline*. The play influenced European taste in the late eighteenth century, helping the swing towards romanticism.

Right: The cast of Ramlilla, splendidly masked. The play is part of an epic about the god Rama.

Opposite: An audience enjoying Ramlilla. Indian drama is little known in the West, but Peter Brook produced the nine-hour epic Mahabharata in Avignon and Paris in 1985.

Sri Harsha, born around 590, was a playwright king of Northern India. His *Priyadarsika* is a court comedy, like the finer *Ratnavali*, where a clown keeps the story going. This is a charming play and it was followed by one with a Buddhist theme, *Nagananda*.

Bhavabhuti, who lived around AD 750, was another Sanskrit dramatist. The best and most famous of his plays is *Rama's Later History*, about Rama, a manifestation of the god Vishnu. It followed an earlier play about Rama's triumphs in war and his coronation. Called *The History of Rama*, it is superb in every way and psychologically sound. Many consider it the finest of all works of art about Rama.

China

China's known dramatic history dates back to the eighth century BC, when religious festivals were occasions for song, dance, acrobatics and pantomime. The eighth-century T'ang emperor Ming Huang started an acting school in a pear garden and might be considered the founding father of Chinese drama. Chinese actors are often called 'the children of the pear garden' to this day and regard the ancient king as their patron.

It was not until the thirteenth century that Chinese drama really came into its own, in unusual circumstances, during the Yuan dynasty. The unfortunate intelligentsia could no longer enter the civil service, which the Mongols had abolished. Reduced to a status little better than prostitutes, they took to acting, performing in and outdoors. Illustrations show a marked likeness to an Elizabethan theatre.

Right: A Chinese spectacle, The Sun and the Moon *staged in the open air. Temples and palaces also served as theatres.*

The most popular dramatist of a later period, the Yuan dynasty, was Kuan Han-Ch'ing, born in the thirteenth century. He is still regularly performed. Eighteen of his plays survive, the most loved of which is *Snow in Midsummer*, whose unfortunate heroine is wrongly condemned to death for a murder she did not commit.

Japan

The most theatrically conscious of the great nations of Asia, Japan has a wide variety of theatrical forms. One has only recently come to light at Oe on the island of Kyushu, a dignified, though less ranging cousin of the famous *noh* plays,

which had been forgotten on the mainland.

Bugaku dates back to seventh-century China. It is a mask play with music and dancing, stemming from religious beliefs. The far more famous *noh* plays had developed by the eighth century, but it was not until the fourteenth that the *noh* theatre reached its classic form, since when it has hardly changed. It was originally an honour ritual for the warriors and nobles. Performances are given on a raised platform some eighteen feet square, with two to six actors as a rule, the principal ones being the *shite* and his friends the *tsure*. A secondary character is the *waki*. An extra character,

*Below: Another splendid
glimpse of a* kabuki *play.*

the *ahi*, may appear, also a child, the *korata*. All the actors are men and are trained from an early age. Highly coloured rich costumes are worn, the *shite* and *tsure* having superb masks. Themes are well-known folk legends. The acting is conventionalized and so largely inaccessible to the uninitiated.

Kabuki is a more popular and accessible form which originated in the seventeenth century as an off-shoot from *noh*. It is still all-male but masks are not worn. Stage hands change the elaborate scenery in full view of the audience. They are regarded as invisible. There is also *joruri*, a puppet-theatre from the seventeenth century as well. The puppets are two-thirds life-sized and fully articulated. The puppeteers can be seen, wearing black, and are again regarded as invisible and the performances include music and song. *Bunraku*, founded in 1871, has life-size puppets.

These are the main forms of Japanese theatre, but there are many others, also stagings of Western plays, making the capital Tokyo theatrically one of the most varied cities on earth.

Left: A striking picture of a kabuki *play and its* audience. Kabuki *players are not masked. Note the musicians.*

Below: Bunraku, *a classical form of a Japanese puppet play.*

The THEATRE REBORN

The German dramatist, poet and historian Hrotsvitha ranks as a heroine of the theatre: she is the first known playwright to emerge in the West after the Dark Ages, and also the first known woman playwright.

This little-known theatrical heroine lived from around 935 to 1001 and wrote at Gandersheim, where she was a nun. Her six short plays, written in Latin, range from comedy to tragedy. Though chastity is her standard theme, the plays are by no means narrow ones. She knew Terence, though her plots are drawn from Christian history, legends and tradition. She has been staged in modern times.

The Church

The very beginnings of church drama stem from around 900, just before Hrotsvitha was born. By about 970 Aethelwold, Bishop of Winchester, was writing about how the Easter story should be performed dramatically in church.

Church drama developed as a means of conveying bible stories to the illiterate. At first the Christmas and Easter stories were acted by priests in the church itself. In the Easter play a cross was set against the north wall of the nave to symbolize the high altar. On the left as the people saw it were the Sepulchre and Heaven and on the right Prison and Hell. Those

Right: Mystery Plays were for the people. Bill Bryden's Mysteries *for the National Theatre have proved how viable they still are.*

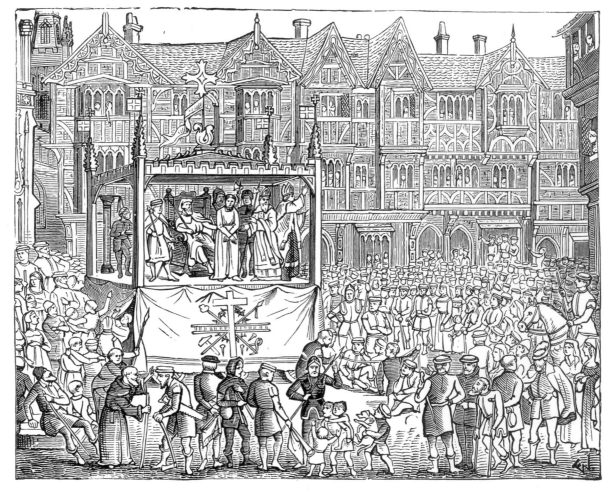

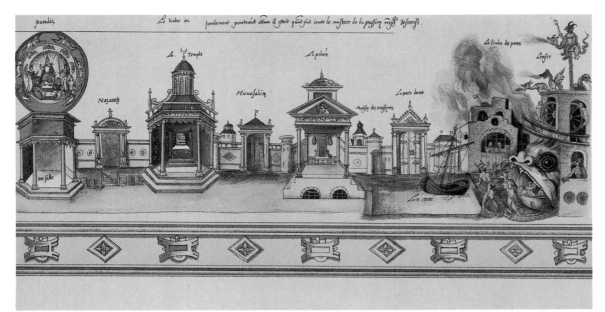

associated with Heaven were on the left, with Hell on the right.

Soon the popularity of the plays made it necessary to take them outside so that more people could see them. The staging remained much the same: the various positions were lined up in front of the audiences and called 'mansions', and the action took place at each of them in turn.

Gradually costumes got more splendid and so did the scenic effects. Hell's Mouth was highly decorated. The Church banned the clergy from taking part, so the local people became the actors, and sometimes wandering players became involved.

These plays were called Miracle, Mystery and, later, Morality plays. 'Miracles' and 'Mysteries' were synonymous in England and were usually organized by the trades guilds. All the actors were male. Texts became more elaborate and sequences of Mystery Plays were created, performed by guild members. The shipwrights would stage a drama about the building of Noah's Ark and the mariners one about the Flood, for instance. It was a matter of prestige for a guild to excel. A cycle of plays lasting a day might be given. The actors were paid a little money, but professional entertainers may well have helped out with special parts. The one early picture we have of a mystery play shows how lively performances were.

Costumes were elaborate, with demons wearing the skins of wolves or of domestic animals. Horns, animal heads, wigs, beards, masks … 'no expense spared'! Adam and Eve sometimes wore white leather to suggest nudity. Colours had associations, the murderer Cain being in red, green Truth and white being

31

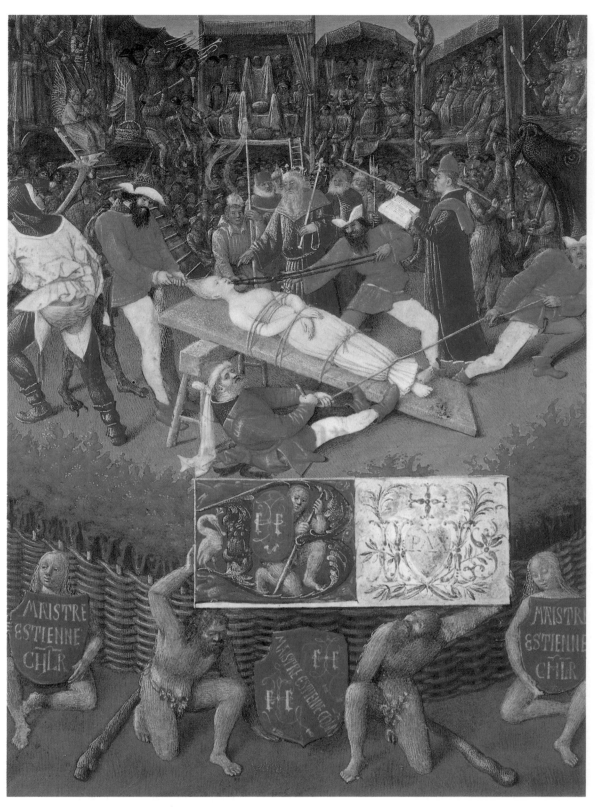

Right: A Mystery Play, The Martyrdom of St. Apollonia. Note the director with a prompt book and wand.

associated with Abel and with Mercy.

There is evidence that some professionals – descendants of the wanderers who had kept theatre alive – took certain leading parts, which must have improved the comic scenes and helped develop the tradition of the Fool.

Realism was sought. Bladders filled with animal blood were used for torture scenes. One Christ almost died on the Cross and a Judas nearly died also by hanging himself a little too efficiently.

In the fifteenth century the bible stories were joined by the Moralities. These were presented on fixed stages and featured anthropomorphic virtues, vices and conditions, such as Mercy, Mischief and Good Deeds. *Everyman*, which dates from the 1490s, is the most famous English Morality. The borderline between professional and amateur seems by this time to have become very blurred.

France introduced the Interlude during the fourteenth century, followed by the rest of Europe soon after. It was a direct descendant of the Roman *mimi* and was played for a nobleman as part of a banquet. Professional actors performed on a raised platform at the end of the hall and settings and costumes were simple.

Left: Characters in a
German Morality Play.
Parts in such plays
included Disgrace, Good
Fame and Wit.

Left: Oberammergau's
famous Passion Play is
performed once every 10
years by the townspeople.

Renaissance

The Renaissance – the revival of interest in classical Greece and Rome in the fourteenth to the sixteenth centuries – resulted in new forms of theatre in Italy and France. Not that performances of the Mystery plays ceased: they continued until the mid-sixteenth century. But now plays by Terence and Plautus were performed, some as early as the fourteenth century, in makeshift theatres based on Roman ones. However, scenically they were understandably more like the Mystery Cycles.

The publication in 1484 of a work from 15 BC, *De Architectura*, revealed to Italians what the Greek Theatre had been like. This naturally affected views on theatre buildings and sets. At the same time there were major developments in art, one of which concerned the use of perspective. At Ferrara in 1508 a backcloth depicting a landscape and buildings with a convincing illusion of depth and also distance is the first recorded use of perspective in the theatre.

The next advance came in 1551 with Sebastiano Serlio's *L'Architettura*, in which he visualized a semi-circular auditorium and a rectangular stage in two parts. Acting would take place on the forepart, scenery would be set towards the back and the rear of the stage raked upwards. Behind it was a painted backcloth and wooden or canvas houses could be placed in front of the backcloth. It was a blend of classical and medieval.

Next came two great theatres, both of which survive to this day in magnificent

Below: An Italian comedy viewed from the stage. The classics were revived in the Renaissance theatre.

COLISEVS SI VE THEATRVM

34

Left: The first proscenium arch is at the Teatro Farnese in Parma (1618). A curtain of the Roman type was used.

Left: Designs by Serlio for stage sets. Left to right: Scena tragica, Scena satyrica, Scena comica, in his Libro secondo di Architettura, *1547.*

Overleaf: The Teatro Olimpico at Vicenza showing Vincenzo Scamozzi's perspective views. He completed the theatre in 1584, Andrea Palladio having started it.

VIRTVTI
OLYMPICOR ACA
A FVNDAM
ANN MDLXXX

Sig.ra Lucia · Trastullo ·

Above: Two of the many characters inspired by the commedia dell'arte, Lucia and Trastullo.

Opposite: The most famous of all commedia dell'arte characters, Arlecchino.

form. The first was the Teatro Olimpico at Vicenza, built between 1580 and 1585 by Palladio and Scamozzi. It was a permanent structure, with a semi-circular auditorium and a very elaborate stone wall behind the raised acting area. There were three doors in the wall painted with perspective views.

In 1619 came another breakthrough, the first proscenium arch, in the Teatro Farnese in Parma. A curtain of the Roman type was used and the actors could now perform on the entire depth of the stage instead of only the portion in front of the scene buildings. The design profoundly affected the future of the theatre.

Spectacular effects were possible at these and later theatres. Scenes could be changed simply by sliding one painted piece in front of another. Winches and rollers produced moving areas, trap-doors were exploited, clouds came and went, chariots rose and descended, and for the first time lighting was used as a theatrical effect, rather than merely illuminating the proceedings. Lanterns and candles now added atmosphere to the action.

Something of the old Roman *mimi* had survived, and out of these and the new surge of interest in theatre came the *commedia dell' arte* improvised plays. The actors played stock characters, Arlecchina, Arlecchino, Pulcinella, Pantalone and others, complete with distinctive costumes. Dialogue was improved, and the plays were usually given on simple stages – the raised platforms and backcloth that was all that was ultimately needed to stage a play.

Meanwhile news of Serlio's work had travelled far and wide. There are records of a performance in 1566 in England on a stage very much along the lines that Serlio recommended. However, the first true English theatre, only ten years away in 1566, would be a very different shape.

Mr ELLER as HARLEQUIN. [SECOND POSITION.] Nº 30.

Drawn and Engraved under the Superintendence of Thos Eblj

Published by M. & M. SKELT. 11. Swan St. Minories. London.

The Age of
SHAKESPEARE

William Shakespeare was born in Stratford-upon-Avon in 1564: if he had been born only half a century earlier he would surely never have achieved a tenth of his universal fame, for a number of crucial reasons.

There were no playhouses in England – the first was built in 1576 – and few professional actors. The English language had not yet reached its apogee of exhilarating, aspiring glory. Also, there was no blank verse.

This marvellous, flexible form did not appear in print until 1557. It was the creation of the Earl of Surrey, who used it in his *Certain Bokes of Vergiles Aeneis* in an attempt to match the grandeur of Virgil's hexameters.

Elizabethan theatre

It is possible to be too carried away by the glory of Elizabethan England, however much one knows of the harsh realities of life for most of its citizens – possible but excusable. The Elizabethans acquired the Renaissance spirit late, and the result was an artistic explosion, especially in drama and dramatic poetry. The dashing Mercutio in *Romeo and Juliet* is Renaissance Man in all his dazzling splendour.

A favourite word of the Elizabethans was 'ravished', and all classes – for the only time in the history of the English stage – were ravished by poetic drama. They revelled in the great Richard Burbage from his first triumph as Richard III onwards, and many of the same people revelled in bear-baiting. It was a world where witches were believed in – and burnt. London was the very heart of this world, and it appears time and again in Elizabethan and Jacobean plays, though

Shakespeare also wrote magically of his native Warwickshire, masquerading as Sicily or a wood near Athens.

Posterity has marvelled how Shakespeare and his theatre came about. The greatest theatre needs a combination of great audience, and great plays and acting. At its greatest, the plays – a reasonable number of them – must be new. This ideal trinity seems to have coincided in Ancient Greece and certainly did so with opera in nineteenth-century Italy, with Verdi's span of works displaying a Shakespearean progression, and gaining huge popularity with all classes. Yet above all it happened in Elizabethan and Jacobean England.

The need for great acting must be stressed as far as the great roles are concerned. Teamwork, so rightly demanded today – the all-important ensemble – is not enough in the greatest dramas. Every regular playgoer has unhappy memories of what happens when an Othello or a Coriolanus is undercast. Fortunately for the Elizabethan audiences, Christopher Marlowe had Edward Alleyn for his leading man and Shakespeare had the incomparable Richard Burbage.

As for their audiences, it has been calculated that 21,000 Londoners, one in eight of the population, went to the theatre every week. There has been nothing to equal those figures in Britain or elsewhere except during the high noon of the cinema which ended in the 1950s.

Early in Queen Elizabeth I's reign (1558–1603) there was no sign of impending greatness. The most important early Elizabethan plays were acted by amateurs, notably *Ralph Roister Doister*, the first English Renaissance comedy, which was possibly first performed in

Opposite: William Shakespeare, a painting attributed to John Taylor c.1610.

40

Right: Edward Alleyn, the first actor to play Marlowe's Tamburlaine and Faustus, and Barabas in The Jew of Malta.

1563. Its author, Nicholas Udall, an Oxford scholar who became headmaster of Eton, had his pupils act this rollicking comedy, which was inspired by his love of Plautus and Terence and would influence the next generation of English writers of comedy. In 1561 law students of London's Inner Temple performed *Gorboduc*, a Renaissance tragedy by Thomas Norton and Thomas Sackville, while *Gammer Girton's Needle* – she lost it – is a comedy featuring English characters that dates from the same time. Its authorship has been disputed, but the needle is finally found in the seat of the breeches of Hodge, the Gammer's manservant, the said Hodge becoming aware of it. The play had its première in Cambridge.

Boy actors were popular until the early years of the seventeenth century, the best known in Elizabeth's reign being the children of the Chapel Royal and St. Paul's. They seem to have been excellent, though the public did not see their efforts until the 1570s, when they appeared at the Blackfriars. They were popular enough to be sneered at by Hamlet.

Meanwhile, professional actors – strolling players – had been touring since the 1400s presenting moral stories and low farces. By Elizabethan times, with the Puritans gaining power and disapproving of pleasure, actors found themselves classed as vagabonds. Only by becoming a great nobleman's servants could they escape a whipping. For their patrons they acted on special occasions and at other times performed in yards, halls and market-places. The best known troupe was the Earl of Leicester's Men, who were to occupy the first English playhouse in 1576.

Theatre buildings

One of the troupe was James Burbage, the great Richard's father. It was he who built the Theatre, inspired by the inn yards that the actors had used and would still use on tours. The players raised a platform on which to perform. Only one drawing of an Elizabethan theatre's interior exists, that of the Swan Theatre in London, and even that is a copy of a lost original. For all that, it remains crucially important. Its accuracy has been challenged, but it has spawned a whole Shakespearean industry.

After the Theatre came the Curtain, Rose, Swan and the legendary Globe, built in 1599, the first two north of the

THE SWAN THEATRE

river, the rest on the south bank. All were 'liberties' beyond the city's jurisdiction. The Theatre was by Finsbury Fields, the Globe on the south bank of the Thames. Some of the hostility to theatres was because they increased the risk of the spread of plague, but the main objection was narrowly religious. One holy man wrote: 'Behold the sumptuous theatre houses, a continual monument of London's prodigality and folly ... The cause of plagues is sin, if you look to it well; and the cause of sin are plays; therefore the cause of plagues.' (Massachusetts would suffer from the same sort of preachers half a century after Shakespeare's death.)

The immortal Globe Theatre, whose architecture is so little documented that

Above: The Swan Theatre, a copy of an original by a Dutch student. A mere impression, but a vital picture. It is unique.

arguments have raged down the centuries about it, was built by the sons of James Burbage in 1599, using timbers from the Theatre. When its lease ran out Cuthbert Burbage, who had failed to negotiate a new one, pulled it down and took the wood across the river to the south bank.

The Globe was owned by its actor-shareholders. All were expected to be singers and they were also expected to dance. The Fools – so hard to play today because their dialogue so rarely seems funny to us – were not so very different from those of the *commedia dell' arte*. Some of the Fools live on in theatre history, notably Richard Tarleton and Will Kempe. As for the boy actors – women were not allowed to act by the Puritans – they must have been very good or Shakespeare would never have

Right: William Kempe was one of Shakespeare's colleagues. He was the first Dogberry in Much Ado. He made his 'dance' for a bet.

Kemps nine daies vvonder
Performed in a daunce from
London to Norwich.

*Containing the pleaſure, paines and kinde entertainment
of William Kemp betweene London and that Citty
in his late Morrice.*

*Wherein is ſomewhat ſet downe worth note; to reprooue
the ſlaunders ſpred of him: many things merry,
nothing hurtfull.*

Written by himſelfe to ſatisfie his friends.

LONDON
Printed by *E. A.* for *Nicholas Ling,* and are to be
ſolde at his ſhop at the weſt doore of Saint
Paules Church. 1 6 0 0.

entrusted great parts to them. Once however, he daringly allowed this dramatic irony in *Antony and Cleopatra*:
I shall see
Some squeaking Cleopatra boy my greatness
I'the posture of a whore.

Most of Shakespeare's plays were first performed at the Globe. It burnt down in 1612 during the première of *Henry VIII*, when a gunshot set fire to the thatch. Everything was burnt within an hour, one man 'having his breeches set on fire, that would perhaps have boiled him, if he had not by the benefit of a provident wit put it out with a bottle of ale'. A second Globe was rapidly built, to be destroyed by the Puritans in 1644.

In 1596 James Burbage converted part of the Blackfriars Priory into a private theatre. Though he died before the conversion was complete, Richard and his brother Cuthbert finished their father's task. Cuthbert became part owner of the Globe and the Blackfriars, Richard becoming the leading actor of the Lord Chamberlain's Men. They would become the King's Men in 1603, the year that King James I, a patron of the theatre to a greater extent than Elizabeth, came to the throne. He was interested in

witchcraft which made him very receptive to *Macbeth*.

Richard Burbage, born in about 1567, was the company's landlord. More importantly, he was the most fortunate actor in the entire history of the theatre, for he was the first to play Richard III, Othello, King Lear and Hamlet, Ferdinand in *The Duchess of Malfi* and other magnificent roles. Tradition and gossip has Shakespeare himself playing character roles like the Ghost in *Hamlet* and Adam in *As You Like It*, perhaps also kings and dukes.

In the theatres the groundlings, often known as stinkards by the middle and upper classes, stood in the open facing the stage, which was some 40 feet square. The buildings were round or polygonal. Only the Fortune is well documented, its contract having survived. The theatres were brightly painted inside.

Arguments will probably never cease about the exact nature of Elizabethan stages unless there is a miraculous find. The stage itself was perhaps five feet high. It had trap doors, entrances and exits being made through upstage doors on the right and the left. There was an inner stage between the doors, probably curtained

Above: The frustrating view of the Globe Theatre in Hollar's Long View of London, *published in 1647.*

45

off (or so most scholars agree, though not the late Dr. Leslie Hotson and his disciples). The inner stage could be used for prison bedrooms etc. Behind it there was a tiring house – the dressing room. The upper stage could serve as a balcony or battlements. However, the Hotson faction have the tiring house under the stage and claim that there was no inner stage and that therefore the great Globe was theatre-in-the-round.

The roof that projected over the stage was known as 'the Heavens' and was supported by two pillars. Below the stage was 'Hell'. A trap door in the Heavens allowed machinery to let down scenery or special effects, and somewhere above the stage the musicians – Elizabethans were

Below: Richard Burbage, the first to play Hamlet, Lear, Richard III, Othello and other great roles.

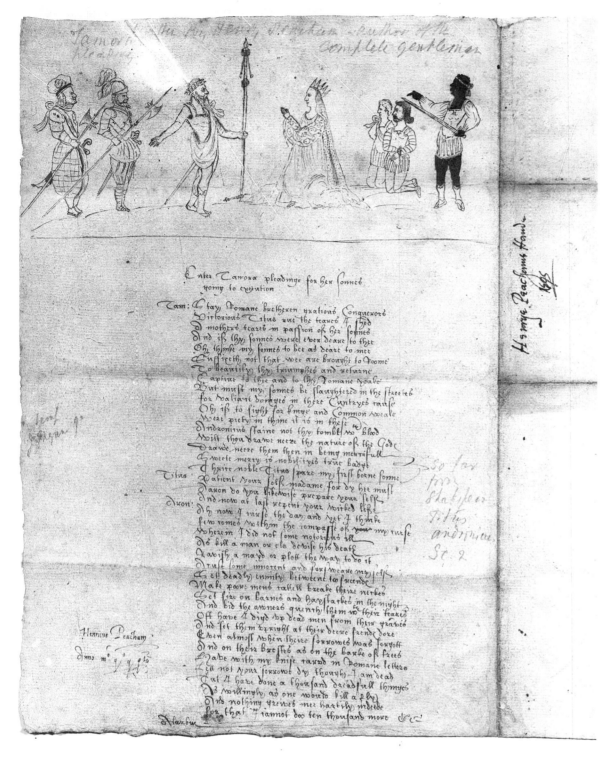

Left: A contemporary drawing of a scene from Titus Andronicus, *giving a valuable glimpse of the play's costumes. Aaron the Moor can be seen, also part of the play.*

'ravished' by music – played from a gallery. Above all else was a turret from which a flag flew on performance days. There was a two o'clock start, three trumpet blasts letting people know a little earlier that it was time for them to take their places. Performances may have been later in the private theatres.

Scenery was basic – as it often is once again today. There were special effects. Costumes were fine and properties were plentiful. Plays were given in contemporary dress, but with a suggestion of period – a plumed helmet for a Roman or a Greek etc. Yet what mattered most were the words. The Elizabethans were word drunk. Poetry was for many heightened living. Shakespeare's apology at the start of *Henry V*, wondering if his stage could 'hold the vasty fields of France' was a rhetorical question. It could.

Plays were essentially working scripts within a company and became the joint property of the company. Sometimes they were pirated during a performance and published. It was just as well that Shakespeare was part of a company, with shares in it, and responsible for staging plays. All plays had to be passed by the censor in case they contained seditious matter. Companies sometimes went on tour, especially in plague years, and such tours must have been gruelling – especially for the strolling companies constantly on tour. Yet references to the actor's lot in Shakespeare need not be taken too seriously. Only in the sonnets does he occasionally bemoan the actor's life so strongly as to suggest a very black mood and in Sonnet III he is almost ashamed of his trade. (Even as late as the end of the Victorian era actors were still being snubbed from time to time.)

Theatre audiences in Elizabethan times were probably some 2,000 to 3,000 strong. The drawing of the interior of the Swan must not be taken as realistic. The size of the Globe's stage is now thought to be comparable with those of the largest opera houses.

Marlowe

Theatrically, 1587 was a tremendous year, for that was the year that the first great English play was performed, Christopher Marlowe's epic, *Tamburlaine the Great*.

Christopher Marlowe (1564–93), the son of a Canterbury shoemaker, was the first playwright to enthrall Elizabethan audiences. It was he who transformed blank verse into his own beautiful and often stupendous 'mighty line', as Ben Jonson called it.

Mighty it certainly was. Not the hero but the Soldan of Egypt delivers this explosive stuff, which should be read out loud:

Right: Donald Wolfit as Tamburlaine at the Old Vic in 1951, directed by Tyrone Guthrie. An epic occasion.

Opposite: Cedric Hardwicke as Dr. Faustus with the Old Vic at the New Theatre in 1948. Robert Eddison is the Mephistopheles.

48

Awake, ye men of Memphis! hear the clang
Of Sythian trumpets; hear the basilisks,
That, roaring, shake Damascus' turrets
  down!
The rogue of Volga holds Zenocrate,
The Soldan's daughter, for his concubine,
And, with a troop of thieves and vagabonds,
Hath spread his colours to our high
  disgrace,
While you, faint-hearted base Egyptians,
Lie slumbering on the flowery banks of Nile,
As crocodiles that unaffrighted rest
While thundering cannons rattle on their
  skins.

Educated at Cambridge, Marlowe is a shadowy figure whose life ended in a tavern brawl. An unrepentant atheist at a time when it was dangerous to be one, and, possibly, killed because of his other profession, the secret service, he lacked Shakespeare's ability to create characters in depth and also lacked humour. Despite that, he was a great playwright who in his short career did far more than pave the way for Shakespeare. It was he who transformed blank verse into an instrument of power and passion. As well as giving audiences his 'mighty line' he thrilled them with extreme lyrical splendour.

Tamburlaine the Great (1587–88) followed an earlier play, *Dido, Queen of Carthage*, closely based on Virgil. The former is an epic about a superman, a hero who is flawed by lust for power and not, as in earlier English tragedies, a great man who 'falls'. (Its influence can be compared only to that of John Osborne's *Look Back in Anger*. The latter did not capture the public as *Tamburlaine* did, but its influence was almost as profound.) Born in the same year as Shakespeare, Marlowe was assessed by the poet Swinburne as 'the greatest discoverer, the most daring pioneer, in all our poetic literature'. In fact, Shakespeare parodied his rival and his actors, notably with Pistol and his overcharged verse, but he undoubtedly loved the work of his only real rival, the man whom he later called 'Dead shepherd'.

Marlowe's later plays include *The Jew of Malta*, in which his Jew is a shallower and less human creation than Shakespeare's Shylock, the play being a virtual horror comic, but very stageable. Fortunately, his masterpiece, *Edward II*, survives. It is both chronicle play and tragedy, a bleak commentary on humanity and power. The extremely lyrical *Doctor Faustus* marks the true dawn of English tragedy. It is shot through with extreme lyricism. Shakespeare parodied Faustus's efforts at magic in the confrontation between Glendower and Hotspur in *Henry IV Part I*. The Elizabethan Theatre was a small competitive world. It was a cruel fate that deprived it of Shakespeare's most notable rival when he was only in his twenties. His only other play is *The Massacre at Paris* – the Massacre of St. Bartholomew's which survives in an extremely corrupt form.

Shakespeare

In Shakespeare's own day he was one of a group of masters. His fellow actors seem to have loved him, not least, no doubt, because he wrote them such wonderful parts. He seems to have been confined to lesser roles – the Droeshout picture suggests a character actor – fortunately for the actors who depended on him, and for posterity. We may surely assume that his fellow actors did their best to see that his main activity was providing good plays for all of them. (Baconians and other amateurs base their arguments on ignorance, incomprehension of the nature of creativeness and the sheer mystery of genius, and also the most arrant snobbery – for Shakespeare, like many of our great playwrights, did not go to a university. Besides his devoted colleagues, sane and sensible men, knew that Shakespeare wrote Shakespeare.)

'Let but Falstaffe come,' wrote Leonard Digges, and the theatre would be packed. Kenneth Tynan once called the two parts of *Henry IV* the twin summits of Shakespeare's achievement, and wrote of great public plays when a whole nation is under scrutiny and on trial. Space forbids more than one example of Shakespeare's mastery, and the *Henry IV* plays provide it. Added to Tynan's tribute are the three versions of Honour, Prince Hal's pragmatic, Falstaff's a mere 'scutcheon' – a nameplate or shield with armorial bearings – and he'll have none of it; Hotspur's honour, on the other hand is something which can be plucked from 'the pale-faced moon'. Shakespeare's boundless humanity and understanding present them all for our inspection. He loves two of the men, both flawed in different ways, but respects the colder Prince Hal, who will one day be Henry V. Falstaff is a pleasure-seeker, an entertaining soak in whom the life-force flourishes mightily. It flourishes in a different way in

Opposite: The title page of the First Folio edition of Shakespeare's plays (1623), with Martin Droeshout's engraving of him.

Mr. WILLIAM
SHAKESPEARES

COMEDIES,
HISTORIES, &
TRAGEDIES.

Published according to the True Originall Copies.

Martin Droeshout sculpsit London.

LONDON
Printed by Isaac Iaggard, and Ed. Blount. 1623.

Speech bubbles in image: "Sir John, art thou there my Deer, my Male Deer?" / "Give me a Cup of Sack — a plague of Sighing & Grief it blows a Man up like a Bladder" / "Base is the Slave that pays" / "When shall we three meet again"

Above: The Shakespeare Jubilee in 1769 was organized by David Garrick to celebrate the great man, not an anniversary. In this procession people are portraying characters. Three days of rain almost ruined the venture.

Hotspur, the volcanically attractive fighting man who, with his companions, starts a civil war. When Shakespeare was born, however, there were those alive who remembered the Wars of the Roses. Whatever his feelings, Shakespeare knew that Prince Hal was the man the country needed. For Elizabethans Henry V was a supreme hero figure.

One other point must be noted even in the shortest account of Shakespeare, the supreme man of the theatre. This is the steady development of his verse. In *Romeo and Juliet* (1595?), though there is wonderful verse, some of it is merely decorative. Benvolio strides on and says: Madam, an hour before the worshipped sun peer'd forth the golden window of the east. Within two years at the most – in *Henry IV Part I* – Shakespeare displays a new and astounding flexibility. The following is blank verse as the vehicle for

characterization of the highest order, Hotspur being the angry speaker:

Why, look you, I am whipp'd and scourg'd with rods
Nettl'd, and stung by pismires, when I hear
of this vile politician, Bolingbroke.
In Richard's time – what do ye call the place?
A plague upon't – it is in Gloucestershire; –
'Twas where the madcap duke his uncle kept,
His uncle York; where first I bow'd my knee
Unto this king of smiles, this Bolingbroke,
'Sblood!
When you and he came back from Ravenspurgh.

After such speeches Shakespeare must have felt that anything was possible. It was. Towards the end of Enobarbus's description of Cleopatra, that ultimate aria – totally justified because we need the description of the queen's meeting with

The Workes of William Shakefpeare,

containing all his Comedies, Hiftories, and

Tragedies: Truely fet forth, according to their firft
ORJGJNALL.

The Names of the Principall Actors
in all thefe Playes.

William Shakefpeare.

Richard Burbadge.

John Hemmings.

Auguftine Phillips.

William Kempt.

Thomas Poope.

George Bryan.

Henry Condell.

William Slye.

Richard Cowly.

John Lowine.

Samuell Croffe.

Alexander Cooke.

Samuel Gilburne.

Robert Armin.

William Oftler.

Nathan Field.

John Underwood.

Nicholas Tooley.

William Eccleftone.

Jofeph Taylor.

Robert Benfield.

Robert Goughe.

Richard Robinfon.

Iohn Shancke.

Iohn Rice.

Antony to understand the plot – Shakespeare, the supreme master, breaks the magical spell with an earthy comment from Agrippa about a previous episode:
Royal wench!
She made great Caesar lay his sword to bed;
He plough'd her, and she cropp'd.
Antony and Cleopatra is usually dated 1606–7, and it is worth noting that Shakespeare's supreme masterpieces, *Hamlet* apart, are strictly speaking Jacobean, as *Othello, King Lear, Macbeth* and *Antony and Cleopatra* appeared after Elizabeth I's death.

The effect that Shakespeare had on audiences is described by Digges, who revealed also how poor Ben Jonson had not the same success:
oh how the Audience
Were ravish'd, with what wonder they went hence
When some new day they would not brooke a line,
of tedious (though well laboured) *Catalines*;
... when let but Falstaffe come.
Hall, Poines, the rest you scarce shall have a roome
All is so pestered: let but *Beatrice*

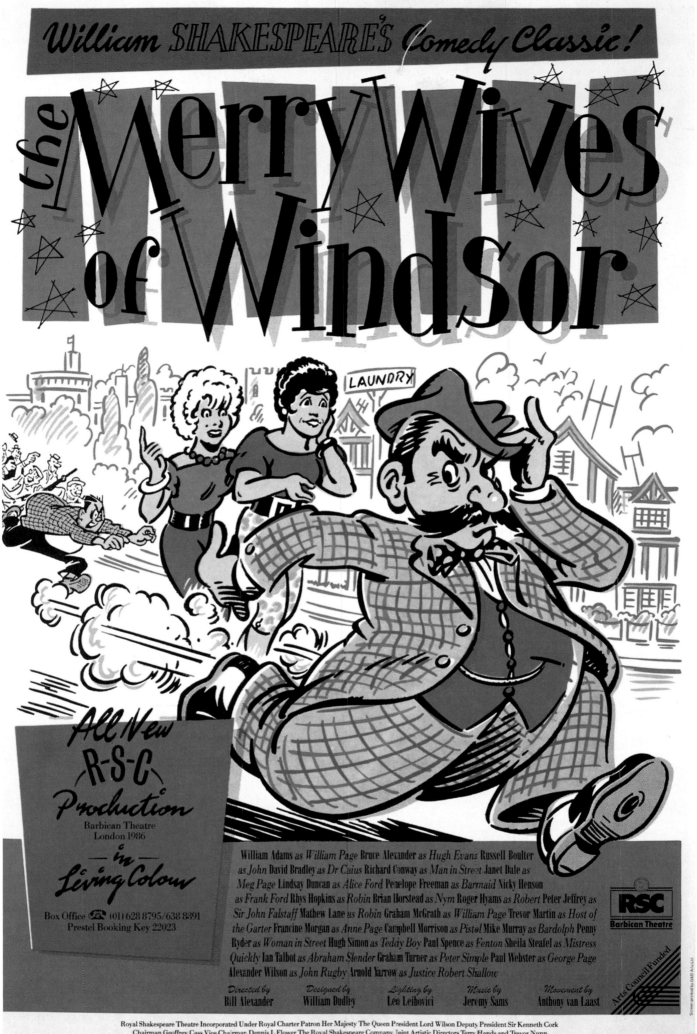

And *Benedicke* be seene, loe in a trice
The Cockpit Galleries, Boxes, all are full
To heare Maluoglio that crosse garter'd
  Gull.

As Shakespeare developed, he must surely have 'lost' some of his audience. Yet Digges shows how he still ravished them:

on tip-toe to reach up
And (from rare silence) clap their brawny
  hands
T'applaud what their charmed soul scarce
  understands.
It should be noted that 'rare' is as in 'O
  rare Ben Jonson'.

Shakespeare's plays are now performed in nearly every country on earth, and in those blessed with good translations of the plays they can be grasped at first hearing even if the incomparable verse is denied the audience. For the English-speaking world some of his vocabulary is inevitably obscure. Directors are rightly very loath to change the scripts (though they may cut them), but just occasionally it is justified. When Peter Brook directed *King John* at Birmingham Rep in 1946, he added five words at the start of the Bastard's great speech on Commodity to explain what the word means today — expediency. It was a rare example of a legitimate insertion, but generally speaking the audience or reader should relax and revel in the entertainment. Homework helps but is essentially an optional extra.

Four Shakespeare plays published in 1600 may have helped pay for building the Globe. None of his manuscripts have survived, but his friends had the plays published in 1623, seven years after his death. The book contains 18 unpublished plays and ranks with the Authorised Version of the Bible as the supreme achievement of the English language.

Shakespeare's supremacy is recognized far beyond the English-speaking world and Europe, but exactly why does he live at the very summit of art? Not by his perfection: he had to work too fast for that. His poetic genius cannot explain it, for millions love him who know no English, let alone Elizabethan English. However, there are explanations beyond argument.

First, he was a born storyteller, a fact of which lesser directors and critics are unaware. In his *Shakespeare's Professional Skills*, Neville Coghill stated that it was his primal starting-point. Shakespeare 'ransacked history and fiction for stories that could be made significant ... He was a supreme storyteller and perceived that the basic source of all meaning that can be presented through his medium was the image of a human action.' He also had a genius for scene-building, while his narrative skill is even more effective because so many of his stories are universal in their appeal.

Added to these was his use of themes: jealousy in *Othello*, pride in *Coriolanus* for example and springing from the stories is the most marvellous array of characters in literature, a teeming throng, even the tiniest parts often having an immortal moment. In *The Winter's Tale* the Third Gentleman tells his friends about the reunion of the two kings and of Leontes and his daughter Perdita. At first the speech is all courtly affectation, then, when describing how Perdita was suddenly overwhelmed by emotion, he goes on '. . . she did, with an "alas!" I would fain say, bleed tears, for I am sure my heart wept blood.'

Again, in *Antony and Cleopatra*, unnamed guards have this exchange towards the play's tragic climax as they hear music:

Fourth Soldier: Peace! What noise?
First Soldier: List, list!
Second Soldier: Hark!
First Soldier: Music i' the air.
Third Soldier: Under the earth.
Fourth Soldier: It signs well, does it not?
Third Soldier: No.
First Soldier: Peace, I say! What should this
  mean?
Second Soldier: 'Tis the god Hercules, whom
  Antony lov'd,
  Now leaves him.

Shakespeare's characters, large and small, spring from his stories and themes and are part of them. Their reality is such that they are part of theatregoers' lives. His range exceeds that of any other dramatist. He draws no saints, perhaps because he did not wish to, perhaps because of censorship, and there is no popular outlaw figure in the plays. Jack Cade in *Henry VI* is fascinating but no hero. For Shakespeare and his contemporaries the bloody Wars of the Roses were recent history. Yet his sympathy with the individual commoner, indeed the individual of all classes, is apparent everywhere. He laughs with, not at, Bottom and his friends, though perhaps the equivalent scene in *Love's Labour's Lost* has a slightly sour edge to it. The other ranks memorably voice their

OUR HONOURED DEAD.

Shakspeare. "TALKING OF POSTERITY—THEY DID SAY SOMETHING ABOUT A NATIONAL THEATRE FOR ME; BUT NOTHING SEEMS TO HAPPEN. WHAT HAVE THEY DONE FOR YOU?"

Milton. "OH, I'M ALL RIGHT. EVERY THREE HUNDRED YEARS THEY GIVE ME A BANQUET AT THE MANSION HOUSE." Shakspeare. "LUCKY DOG!"

opinions before Agincourt in *Henry V.* His message is sometimes put across in ways that would astound him, but, like his Caesar he bestrides the narrow world like a Colossus. He is greatly loved because his own world embraces all humanity. His plays are, as he said of Cleopatra, 'unparallel'd'.

Ben Jonson

Only Ben Jonson among Shakespeare's colleagues seems to have publicly realized this. A quarrelsome, bitter man, his *Volpone* and *The Alchemist* still give delight, as does *Bartholomew Fair*, a bustling, noisy picture of Jacobean London on the spree. *Volpone*, about a cunning old miser, is a brilliant study of gullibility. His tragedies, which are satirical-tragic satires, were not very successful even in his own day. He was born eight years after Shakespeare, but outlived him by many years, dying in 1637.

Other Elizabethan dramatists include Thomas Kyd, whose *The Spanish Tragedy* (1588) inspired a line of revenge tragedies; Thomas Heywood, author of *A Woman Killed with Kindness* (1603), a warmly human domestic drama with strongly drawn characters; and Thomas Dekker's *The Shoemaker's Holiday*, the most

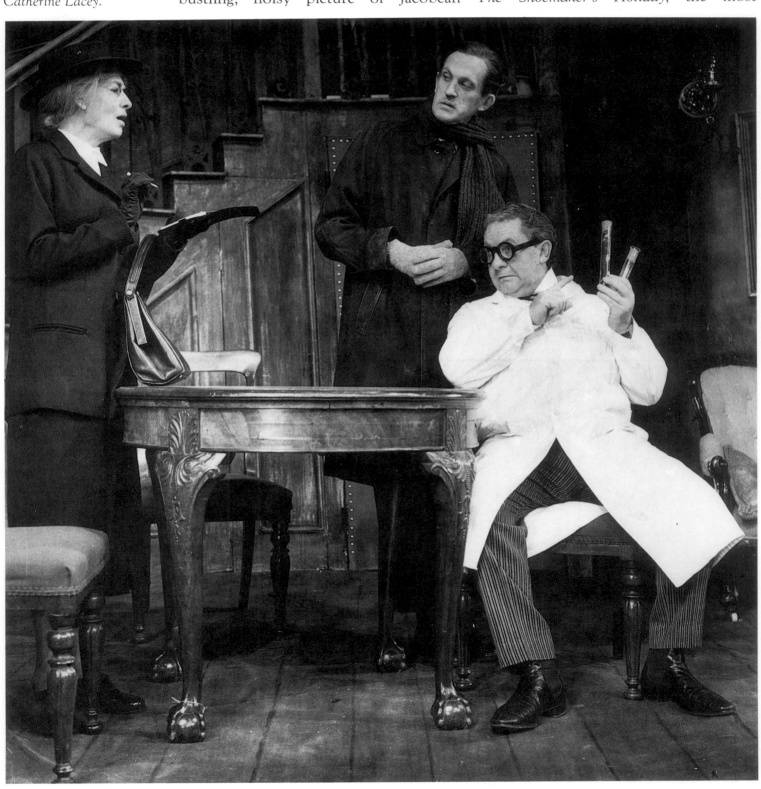

popular of his 40 or so plays. It gives a delightful picture of Londoners even if some of the language is too colloquial to be understood today. The period was so rich in playwrights that space forbids more than a mention of John Fletcher, Francis Beaumont, Philip Massinger, John Ford and Nathan Field, who started as a child star and finished by sharing leads with Burbage. He was a better actor than playwright. It was a period when playwrights regularly collaborated, the best-known pair being Beaumont and Fletcher, masters of romantic tragi-comedies.

Jacobean theatre

Tragedy

Jacobean tragedy has fared fairly well in recent times, its horrors being taken by audiences in their stride. Some of these plays thrill modern audiences not so much because of their horrific plots but because of their pessimistic power. The greatest are both by John Webster, whose life is obscure even by Elizabethan standards. Born around 1580, his masterpieces are *The White Devil* and *The Duchess of Malfi*. (Bernard Shaw foolishly called him the Tussaud Laureate.) His most famous line – from the latter play – has never been bettered: Ferdinand looks down at his dead sister and says: 'Cover her face: mine eyes dazzle: she died young.'

Other extraordinary plays include Cyril Tourner's *The Revenger's Tragedy* and Thomas Middleton's *The Changeling*. These plays were given in indoor theatres, along with some of Shakespeare's. Apart from the obvious advantages of these, the audiences tended to be better educated. The theatres were lit by candles. The second Blackfriars Theatre had the audience sitting on benches. Painted scenery was introduced from Italy, being

Aery Spirit Scogut Scolton Rosicros

FIGURES DESIGNED BY INIGO JONES FOR THE MASQUE OF "THE FORTUNATE ISLES."

Right: Inigo Jones, the artist and architect, was England's first scenic artist, designing many Court masques.

first used in the court masques. These were worlds away from Jacobean drama with its violent plots, complete with rape, incest etc. which, it must be admitted, added fuel to the Puritans' campaign against the theatres.

Masques

Inigo Jones, the architect and designer, was a leading figure in the development of the masque. He had travelled widely in Italy, and seen the theatres at Vicenza and Parma. In 1605 he collaborated with Ben Jonson in *The Masque of Blackness*, which featured a moving 'sea'. Later masques had half a hall used as a stage, and settings became more and more elaborate. The King and Queen, and later King Charles I and his queen, patronized these entertainments, in which the actors were amateurs, often courtiers. As they were private entertainments women were allowed to take part. Masques have been

very unfavourably compared with Jacobean tragedies, yet their imaginative staging and lavish costumes and scenic effects – learnt from the Italians – paved the way for a new kind of theatre which would influence the history not only of drama but of the new arts of opera and ballet.

Meanwhile, politics and puritanism combined to put an end to the age of supreme theatrical glory in the most drastic and effective fashion. The Puritans got their wish to have the London playhouses closed on 2 September 1642, just after the Civil War started. The abandoned theatres were not pulled down at once, indeed, the Blackfriars, where Shakespeare and his colleagues had acted, survived until 1655. The Globe was pulled down on 15 April 1644, 'to make tenements in the room of it'. Yet it will remain the most famous and magical of theatres as long as theatre itself survives.

THEATRICAL EUROPE
From de Vega to Sheridan

Spain

Spain's age of theatrical glory coincided with England's. Her first great playwright, Lope de Vega, was born two years before Shakespeare, and Spanish and English audiences went to theatres that were remarkably alike.

Early Spanish actors performed in the halls of aristocrats, or in *corrales* (yards) between houses. Again there is the similarity between the Spaniards and the Elizabethans performing in innyards. The first Spanish theatres were based on the *corrales*, with the audiences either standing as the groundlings stood in London, or sitting in boxes and galleries. One feature that was completely different from the Elizabeth theatres was that there were special boxes for women. The stage did not 'thrust' out so far as an Elizabethan one, but no Elizabethans would have been surprised by the theatres of Madrid, Valencia and Seville around the year 1600. Happily, one corral theatre of the seventeenth century still exists in Amalgro; it was discovered in the 1960s.

De Vega (1562–1635) claimed that he had written 1,500 plays and a biographer has claimed 2,000 for him. Whatever the truth, fewer than 500 survive, which is still a prodigious output, a torrential one in splendid verse. He was not the first Spanish playwright, but it was he who truly established Spain's professional theatre, helped by the Spaniards, like the English, having an endless appetite for theatre. He excelled in both tragedy and comedy.

This Armada veteran ranged from farce to dramatized lives of the saints and may be said to have invented cloak and dagger drama. His *Fuenteovejuna* (The Sheep Women) is about rebellious villagers and

Above: The corral theatre at Amalgro in Spain, discovered in modern times and now restored.

has been called the first proletarian drama, and the poetic *El Caballero de Olmedo* (The Knight from Olmedo) is still much admired.

De Vega wrote for the Spanish court using all the latest scenic effects. He also wrote *autos sacramentales*, which were acted on three carts, the middle one as the main acting area and the outer ones with machinery on them for special effects.

De Vega had an enemy, a Mexican-born hunchback named Alarcón (1580–1639). The artistic consequence was a series of well-written and bitter plays which found more favour in France than in Spain, notably *La verdad sospechosa* (Truth Itself Suspect). He influenced the great French dramatist Corneille.

Cervantes, author of *Don Quixote*, was also a playwright, whose finest stage works were his comic interludes. His Senecan tragedy *El cerco de Numancia*

(The Siege of Numancia), about a Spanish city besieged by the Romans, has inspired his countrymen at critical moments and the French during the Occupation. Coincidentally, he and Shakespeare died on the very same day.

Tirso de Molina is best remembered for writing the first work about Don Juan.

Pedro Calderón de la Barca (1600–81) is regarded by many as the most remarkable and important Spanish dramatist. He wrote some 200 plays, one of the finest and best known outside Spain being *El Alcalde de Zalamea* (The Mayor of Zalamea). As in so many other Spanish plays honour is at the heart of it – the *pundonor* (point of honour), a deadly serious concept, in the context of *The Mayor of Zalamea* concerning the virginity of his daughter. His plays are tightly written and all his characters have relevance to the plots. None of his religious pieces are dependent on clichés. He wrote comedies, romances, cloak-and-dagger plays, and religious pieces, these last after becoming a priest in 1651.

He became a playwright at 14, was later King Philip IV's Court Playwright, and his influence extended outside Spain, with some of his plays adapted by the English Restoration dramatists from French translations of the original.

By Calderón's time Italian influence, as elsewhere, resulted in magnificent spectacle and perspective scenery in Spanish theatres. He made the most of the new techniques and the results greatly pleased the Court and the aristocracy. Among his other plays are *El magico prodigioso* (The Wonder-Working Magician) inspired by the life of St. Cyprian, and *El médico de su honra* in Roy Campbell's distinguished translation (*The Surgeon of his Honour*).

Late in the seventeenth century the Spanish form of operetta known as *Zarzuela* was originated. Italian opera proved too strong a rival in the eighteenth century, but in the following century it was revived. It can take foreign influences in its stride, musicals included, which has resulted in its survival today.

65

...lière.   Jodelet.   Poisson.   Turlupin.   Le Capitan Matamore.   ...h...   Guillot Gorju.

France

The unities cause constant disputes in France. Her first professional playwright, Alexandre Hardy (c.1575–1631) had written tragi-comedies, but the French literary establishment and most writers kept the 'rules', the classical rules of Aristotle which, as has been noted, they misunderstood in part.

Hardy wrote plays for the first truly professional company of Parisian actors, who performed in the Hotel de Bourgogne, which housed a theatre. He was the resident dramatist. Sadly, he was no genius, but he gave great pleasure. So did his famous farceurs, Gros-Guillaume, Gaultier and Turlupin, French descendants of *commedia dell'arte* players.

French theatres were roofed. The audience stood in the sloping pit or sat on benches further back, and there were boxes on each side. Clearly the standard of acting was high, for when France's golden age of theatre began, the actors – and the audiences – were ready for it.

The French theatre never had anything as lethal as the Puritans to contend with, but its development was hindered by the long civil wars of the sixteenth century, causing it to lag behind England and Spain. All this changed when *Le Cid* by Pierre Corneille (1606–84) had its première in 1636 or 1637, though the plot, complete with *pundonor*, was

Left: One of many Italian actresses to triumph in France seen here in Corneille's Horace.

inspired by Spanish drama. His first play *Mélite*, a farcical comedy, was given in a converted tennis court in 1629. It succeeded despite criticisms that the unities were not obeyed, the most vocal objector being one Jean Mairet who did obey them. Corneille was also accused of leaving out stock farce characters.

Le Cid caused a storm in literary circles, for it was a tragi-comedy. It seemed to observe the unities, but was more exactly a romantic drama disguised as a classic one. Literary circles rarely make true reputations in the theatre, however, and Corneille's genius was recognized. He created tragic, heroic men and women, some of them superhuman, and focused French tragedy on the soul, not simply on actions. The 1640s were his greatest years, his plays including *Horace*, *Cinna*, *Polyeucte*, *La Mort de Pompée* and the

Below: Molière, the total man of the theatre.

comedy *Le Menteur*. His Pompey play drew parallels between Ancient Rome and the political upheavals of the reigns of Louis XIII. His later plays were less remarkable, and Racine gradually overtook him in popularity. Both wrote a play about Bérénice, Queen of Palestine, which stirred literary circles. Molière's wife Armande Béjart played the role in Corneille's version. Corneille, unlike Racine, reserved his best roles for men, his finest female roles being strong ones – Medea and Cleopatra – but his less powerful women, notably Pauline in *Polyeucte*, are gratefully taken by major actresses. In his own lifetime he was hailed and known as *le grand* Corneille. His brother Thomas was also a successful dramatist, one of the incomparable Rachel's roles – nearly two centuries later – being the tragic heroine in *Ariane*.

France's greatest playwright, Molière, was born in 1622. His real name was Jean-Baptiste Poquelin. He was also a manager and a director, a fascinating man, totally of the theatre, who saw to it that comedy became the equal of tragedy in the French theatre. He was also happy to antagonize, writing a play called *Impromptu de Versailles* in which he criticized the actors of the rival Hotel de Bourgogne company for their exaggerated declamatory style. It helped that he had King Louis XIV as a patron.

Before considering Molière the playwright, the great man as director must be shown in action. Here are some of his comments to his own company: Endeavour then, all of you, to take the Character of your Parts right, and to imagine that you are what you represent. (To Du Croisy) You play the Poet, and you ought to fill yourself with that Character, to mark the Pedant Air which he preserves even in the Conversation of the Beau Monde; that sententious Tone of Voice, and that Exactness of Pronunciation which lays stress on all the Syllables, and does not let one Letter escape of the strictest Orthography. (To Brecourt) As for you, you play a Courtier, as you have already done in *The School for Wives Criticis'd*; that is, you must assume a sedate Air, a natural Tone of Voice, and make the fewest Gestures possible. (To La Grange) As for you, I have nothing to say to you!

There was a considerable middle-class audience in Paris, as well as an upper-class one, members of which could be as boorish as their English counterparts of the period.

Molière had deserted a legal career to become an actor. In 1642 he joined the

Above: Molière breakfasting with his patron Louis XIV at Versailles.

Béjarts, an acting family, then, with Madeleine Béjart, he founded the Illustre-Théâtre. He endured a spell in prison when it ran into debt. He then joined another company and got his training as a dramatist writing short farces for them and also acting in them. In 1658 they performed before the 20-year-old Louis XIV in the Louvre, first presenting a Corneille tragedy. Then Molière came on stage and announced a farce of his own, *Le Docteur amoureux* (The Doctor in Love), which not only revealed his gifts as a playwright, but also his talent for comedy acting. King Louis gave the troupe the right to remain in Paris. They took over the Théâtre du Petit-Bourbon, which they shared with Italian players, who greatly influenced Molière. Later he and his colleagues took over the Théâtre du Palais-Royal.

Tragedies did not prove to be the company's forte, but Molière was ready with comedies. *L'Etourdi* (The Blunderer) and *Le Dépit amoureux* (The Amorous Quarrel) were produced, then came Molière's first great success, *Les Précieuses ridicules*, in 1659. It delighted everyone but the fashionable young, whom it satirized.

This one-acter was followed by a string of masterpieces which the King and the unbiased members of the public adored, thus protecting the company and,

Right: The Comédie-Française production of Tartuffe, *seen at the Aldwych Theatre in 1964 as part of Peter Daubeny's World Theatre season.*

particularly, Molière from the wrath of those he often pilloried and scandalized. His *L'Ecole des Femmes* had prudes and pedagogues raging at him, while his masterpiece *Tartuffe*, which was staged in 1664, exposed religious hypocrisy all too well. Other masterpieces followed, *Le Misanthrope: Le Médecin malgré lui* (The Doctor in Spite of Himself); *L'Avare* (The Miser); *Le Bourgeois gentilhomme*; then his satire on learned ladies, *Les Femmes savantes*. His last play was *Le Malade imaginaire* (The Hypochondriac) in 1672 when the King was beginning to withdraw his support because of religious and political pressures. Molière died on stage in 1673 in this last of his plays. Contrary to legend he was given a Christian burial thanks to good friends, but it was at night to avoid a scandal.

Molière's *Don Juan* was denounced as atheistical and some demanded that the playwright should be burnt. It is worthy of note that between 1680 and 1920, a seventh of the total number of plays presented at the Comédie-Française were by Molière, while *Tartuffe* is never out of the annual repertoire.

It was Molière who raised French comedy to the heights and the prestige of tragedy, though comedy is too weak a word for the work of such a satirist and social commentator. His plays are universal even though they are difficult to translate without losing some of their wit. His verse, his construction and, of course, his flair for comedy are superb. Some of his endings are arbitrary, some of his characters are types rather than individuals, but no-one has more finely delineated character through comedy than he.

France's other great seventeenth-century dramatist was Jean Racine (1639–99). Corneille, said La Bruyère, showed men as they ought to be and

Above: Le Malade Imaginaire *(The Hypochondriac), one of Molière's masterpieces. This is the National Theatre's 1981 production with Daniel Massey in the title role and Emily Morgin as his daughter.*

Right: Jean Racine (1639–99), the great French playwright and poet.

J.RACINE.1673.

Opposite: Glenda Jackson as Phèdre and Gerard Murphy as Theseus in Philip Prowse's 1984 production of Racine's masterpiece, Phèdre.

Racine as they are, oddly meaning this as a criticism of Racine. An unlikable genius, raised by the Jansenists at Port-Royal – their faith resembled the starkness of Calvinism – he was given his first chance in the theatre by Molière, who staged his *La Thébaïde, ou les Frères ennemis* in 1664. Racine then took his play *Alexandre le Grand* from Molière's company and gave it to the company at the Hotel Bourgogne. Molière never spoke to him again. Racine also fell out with the Jansenists, who were hostile to the stage.

His most famous plays are *Britannicus, Bérénice, Bajazet* and, especially, *Phèdre* (1677). This last, one of the great theatrical female roles, combines fate in the Greek sense with a modern person torn apart with guilt yet condemned to evil ways. The play deals with the heroine's love for her husband's son and was apparently written with a deliberately small vocabulary of words. A line of powerful actresses have relished the title-role, the most famous in modern times being Sarah Bernhardt.

Racine ended his life as a Jansenist once again, also as a good husband and Christian. Despite this startling change, he achieved two successful plays on biblical themes, *Esther* and *Athalie*, the latter becoming a pillar of the repertoire of the Comédie-Française.

Phèdre appeared four years after Molière's death. Both events marked the end of a glorious era. It had been a dangerous one, though the King had lessened the danger.

The Comédie-Française

The great theatre, the first of all national theatres, was founded in 1680 by Louis XIV. The company of the Théâtre de Marais had merged with that of the Hotel de Bourgogne, which had absorbed Molière's company in 1673, the year of his death. The present home of the Comédie-Française dates from 1790, though the company did not occupy it until 1799.

The merger of 1680 did not produce great drama. The glorious days – so rare in even the most theatrical nations – were past. The Comédie-Française, for all its fine artists, had an unadventurous repertoire, new dramatists failing to equal the old.

Molière had been very friendly with Tiberio Fiorillo, the leader of a *commedia dell'arte* troupe, who had shared a theatre with his company. Both had gone to the Palais Royal from their old theatres and now the Italians were given permission to act in French. This enraged the Comédie-Française, not least because they often

Opposite: Marie Antoinette dancing in a Court ballet.

Left: Adrienne Lecouvreur, a famous actress of the Comédie-Française who died in her thirties in 1730. Rachel and Bernhardt later acted in a play about her life.

improvised. Worse, Mme de Maintenon, the king's mistress, decided that she had been slighted by the high-spirited Italians in one of their plays and they were banished from the capital until 1716.

When the actors returned they found that Italian was no longer so fashionable and within a few years they were Italian in name only. It was they who performed the comedies of Pierre Marivaux (1688–1763) which were to be more popular in the nineteenth century than in the playwright's day. Mood is more important than plot in Marivaux, whose plays were very different from those of his contemporaries.

The Comédie-Française did not perform Marivaux as well as the Italians did, and it fell out with Alain Le Sage, whose play *Turcaret*, remodelled from an earlier one of his, is one of the finest French comedies. It concerns a tax farmer who has exploited the poor, and was very topical because there was much bitterness over taxation at the time it was produced in 1710. Author and actors were offered bribes to keep it from the stage, but they refused. It remains in the French repertory.

The great philosopher Diderot wrote much better about the theatre than for it, producing second-rate bourgeois dramas, but the even greater Voltaire had more success. An admirer of Shakespeare –

unusual in a Frenchman of his times – his early plays show signs of his admiration. He wrote mainly *drames bourgeoises* and *comedies larmoyantes* (tearful comedies), but they are no longer performed. For all his love of theatre and literary success he had not the spark of theatrical drama in him. Far more interesting is the fact that the beautiful actress Adrienne Lecouvreur, an excellent tragedienne who lives on in dramatic and operatic form, died in his arms. She was not allowed a Christian burial, which provoked him, the most powerful pen in France, to launch a savage attack on the Church.

There was a last glimpse of greatness just before the Revolution broke out in 1789. It was provided by Pierre Beaumarchais (1732–99), destined forever to be overshadowed by Mozart's adaptations of his works, but an important figure in his own right who dared to subject the aristocracy to scathing criticisms.

His other careers included smuggling, espionage, making watches and dealing in finance, also gun-running for the American colonists during the War of Independence. He wrote two plays before his first great success, *Le Barbier de Seville*, which was produced in 1775. The Comédie-Italienne would not stage it because it was considered that the hero was modelled on its star, who had once been a barber himself! After troubles with the censor it was staged by the Comédie-Française. The author ran into infinitely more trouble with his *Le Mariage de Figaro*. The first Figaro play had mocked the aristocracy, but by no means as devastatingly as the second one did. It had its much awaited first night in 1784 and few plays have been so excitedly anticipated. In the event the playwright's outspoken criticism of the aristocracy was inflammatory. It appalled Louis XVI, who called its production a dangerous folly, but it ran for 80 performances, which was unequalled in the eighteenth century. It was a very well-written play, which must be emphasized. Its impact needs no stressing. Happily, the great man did not end up on the guillotine, the destination of so many early revolutionaries. His craftsmanship was considerable, influencing many later French writers including Scribe and Feydeau. His Figaro plays as we have them are diminished by the censor, though it is impossible to say by how much. It does not matter: he succeeded.

England

When the Puritans finally had the theatres closed, English actors either joined the King's Army – the Civil War broke out in 1642 – or took up other trades. A few performances were given in private houses in strict secrecy but one of great interest was not hushed up.

The man who presented it was Sir William Davenant, who claimed to be Shakespeare's son. True or not, he was a

Below: M. Samson, the first Barber of Seville in Beaumarchais's play.

Right: Sir William
Davenant, dramatist,
manager and possibly
Shakespeare's son.

gallant soldier in the Civil War and a
theatrical tower of strength after it.

Oliver Cromwell, a lover of music, had
seen to it that it was not banned by
Puritan extremists. Opera had been
(literally) invented in Florence in 1597 by
a group of enthusiasts, musicians,
scholars and others who hoped to
recapture the mixture of words and music
that they believed had existed in Greek
drama. The first opera resulted in 1597,
Orfeo by Peri, which is now lost. Opera
would find its first genius in Monteverdi a
few years later. Importantly for all
branches of theatre the new art stimulated
Italian designers to glorious feats of scenic
design and effects, which revolutionized
stage design. The diarist John Evelyn was
only one of those who marvelled at the
sheer brilliance of Italian theatricality. At
this period opera led the way, not least in
popularity. Venice alone had ten opera
houses by 1700.

Meanwhile Davenant persuaded the
authorities that opera was a respectable
revival of the classical arts, and in 1656 he
presented *The Siege of Rhodes*, with
singers, not the outlawed actors, on a
small stage at Rutland House. The first
English actress, a Mrs Coleman, appeared
in it. She had already performed in a little
piece called *The First Day's Entertainment*,
also by Davenant. Mrs Coleman ranks as
the first English opera singer as well as the
first actress. Alas, the music, by a number
of composers, has not survived. Dennis
Arundell, in his *The Critic at the Opera*,
suggests that Davenant probably managed to stage some other entertainments,
despite the Puritans.

Restoration drama

Oliver Cromwell, Lord Protector of England, died in September 1658, and, after various political and military crises, the monarchy was restored. Under Charles II the theatre soon revived.

Nearly 20 years had elapsed since the Puritans had closed the playhouses, a generation of theatregoers had died, others had lost the habit and the old theatres had been demolished. However, Charles II was a keen theatregoer, and a patron of the arts – and science – generally, so it took little time to re-establish the theatre, changed as it would be from the Elizabethan one. The audience, too, was different, no longer a cross-section of the population but an upper- and upper-middle-class one, complete with courtiers and assorted hangers-on, ladies of pleasure included. The old open air theatres were replaced with more modern versions of the old indoor ones.

Inevitably, tastes had changed, and even Shakespeare was suspect. He was obviously too great and popular to be banished from the boards, but it was felt that such a primitive barbarian could be improved.

Naturally, the versatile Davenant was the man of the moment. Perhaps praying his (possible) father to forgive him, he and others resorted in *Macbeth* to dancing and singing witches who took to the air as well as the stage, while *Romeo and Juliet* was given a happy ending. In Nahum Tate's rewriting of *King Lear*, it both ended happily and Cordelia and Edgar became lovers. Restoration audiences expected heroic love on stage – and got it. Space forbids discussion of other travesties.

Early Restoration performances took place in old enclosed halls like the Cockpit. A converted tennis court served the King's Men who were under the management of Thomas Killigrew. He had been a page to Charles I and was now Groom of the Bedchamber to his son. After three years Killigrew was able to move to the original Drury Lane, which was opened in 1663 and named the Theatre Royal. Following the Italian fashion it had a pit in front of the stage

Below: The Dorset Garden Theatre premières included Venice Preserv'd *and an operatic* Tempest, The Enchanted Isle.

and an almost circular tier of boxes. Davenant's own company moved to the Dorset Garden Theatre in 1671. There the acting took place in front of the proscenium arch, with lavish scenic effects as backgrounds. Drury Lane was burnt down in 1672, but was soon rebuilt by Sir Christopher Wren. There was a special room under the stage for the machinery for set changes and splendid effects.

These were not large theatres. The mainly upper-class audiences went to be seen as well as to see. There were also additional hazards: Samuel Pepys went to the theatre (as he often did) and later noted in his diary that 'a lady spit backward upon me; but after seeing her to be a very pretty lady I was not troubled at it at all'.

Not surprisingly, the advent of actresses was a huge success. Nell Gwynn, the ex-orange girl, was a favourite, though she is best remembered for her off-stage activities rather than her limited talents.

Mrs Betterton, wife of the great Restoration actor Thomas Betterton, was far finer. Betterton was the leading Shakespearean. His Hamlet terrified his Ghost, Barton Booth. The fact that Betterton was 'an ill figure, being clumsily made' seems not to have mattered.

Interestingly, in early Restoration plays men still took women's parts if necessary because of the shortage of actresses. Edward Kynaston was a notable female impersonator. He must have been very convincing for Pepys said he made 'the loveliest lady that ever I saw in my life'. Fashionable ladies lionized him and on one famous occasion the curtain could not go up, despite the presence of the King, because Kynaston needed a shave. He lived until 1706, having graduated to heroic male parts.

The King would allow only two acting companies in London, both with Royal patents. Davenant was finally established at Lincoln's Inn Fields Theatre, and Killigrew stayed at Drury Lane. There is

no doubt that the fashionable audiences helped inspire Restoration comedy in all its bawdy glory and Restoration tragedy, which now rarely emerges from theatrical bookshelves. Thomas Otway's *Venice Preserv'd* (1682) is virtually the only one still to be staged.

Restoration comedy, which includes plays written over 40 years after King Charles returned, ranges from the robust, entertaining comedies of William Wycherley (1640–1716) to the masterpieces of William Congreve (1670–1729) and George Farquhar (1678–1707). They demand stylish acting: the prose is so masterly that it cries out for perfection of delivery. They remain readily understandable today, as English in the seventeenth century had developed to a form familiar to twentieth-century audiences.

No account can omit five of these comedies. Wycherley's *The Country Wife* has the libertine Horner pretending to be impotent to avert the suspicions of husbands. Congreve's *Love For Love* is funny, witty and joyous, and his *The Way of the World*, which had its première in 1700, is, if anything, even more perfectly written, but has a tortuous plot. For all that, the parts of the hero and heroine, Mirabell and Millamant, touch heights of witty perfection equalled only, perhaps, by Shakespeare's Beatrice and Benedick in *Much Ado About Nothing*.

The last great Restoration dramatist was George Farquhar, the Irish-born creator of two hugely entertaining and lasting comedies, *The Recruiting Officer* and *The Beaux' Strategem*. He is a link between the Restoration and Sheridan, with a warmth that much Restoration drama lacked. His death before he was 30 was a catastrophe, and there followed a period without genius.

Restoration plays came under more and more public censure as the middle classes started going to the theatre once again. The architect and playwright Sir John Vanbrugh, who built Blenheim Palace, provoked a broadside from the pamphleteer Jeremy Collier, whose *Short View of the Immorality of the English Stage* was published in 1698. The offending plays were *The Relapse, or Virtue in Danger* (1696) and *The Provok'd Wife* (1697). The former has a superb creation, Lord Foppington. Collier, however, was not amused by him, and his strictures were such that the great Congreve retired to live as a gentleman. Voltaire was furious

Left: Peter Wood revived his 1965 hit production of Love for Love *at the National Theatre 20 years later. The cast included Michael Bryant and Amanda Redman.*

with him when he paid him a visit, resenting the waste of a genius.

Eighteenth century

If a series of great or good plays is considered the sign of a truly healthy theatre then the theatre of eighteenth-century England might not rank high. Apart from *The Beggar's Opera* (1728), Goldsmith's *She Stoops to Conquer* (1773) and Sheridan's three masterpieces in the 1770s, *The Rivals, The School for Scandal* and *The Critic*, there is not a single play of the period that is regularly staged after *The Beaux' Stratagem* appeared in 1707. Very occasionally David Garrick's *The Clandestine Marriage* is given. Yet the century was very important theatrically.

Many new theatres were built in Georgian times, not too large until late in the century. There were many built outside London across the nation, three of which survive – at Bristol, Richmond in Yorkshire and Margate. Strolling players took their plays around the country, travelling on foot or by wagon. The middle classes – usually the backbone of theatre audiences – began going to the theatre regularly. That bourgeois plays of no great importance were popular – along with Shakespeare – is beside the point. An audience was being brought into being, one that was sometimes privileged to witness true greatness. David Garrick was one of the most famous men of his age and Charles Lamb was able to look back on Sheridan's masterpiece in its morning glory and write: 'Amidst the mortifying circumstances

Below: This marvellous print of strolling players is from an original by Hogarth. Such scenes could still be sometimes found until well into the twentieth century.

Right: Charles Macklin as Shylock, his most famous role.

attendant upon growing old, it is something to have seen *The School for Scandal* in its prime.'

The most remarkable theatrical figure in the early years of the century was John Rich, who built and managed the first Covent Garden Theatre (1732). That extraordinary British institution, pantomime (not to be confused with the silent French version), was popularized by him. He was an excellent Harlequin, anglicizing the *commedia dell'arte* character, notably as Harlequin Jack Sheppard (a notorious highwayman). Until the early years of this century a harlequinade ended every pantomime.

John Gay's *The Beggar's Opera* (1728), 'making Gay rich and Rich gay', as the saying went, was a political satire which is rather obscure today, though shot through with fine and beautiful old English tunes. Handelian operas and others are satirized, including their artificially happy endings, while the highwayman hero Macheath is a satire on Britain's first Prime Minister, Sir Robert Walpole. The topical allusions are lost on modern audiences, but the piece lives on today because of its theatrical flair and lovely melodies. Its première was at Lincoln's Inn Fields, Davenant's old theatre.

David Garrick (1717–79) was born into a family of Huguenot exiles from France, and was taught by the redoubtable Doctor Johnson, accompanying him to London. He later deserted his job in the wine trade for the theatre. Before considering his magnificent career, the stage must be set for him.

The leading actor of the 1720s and 1730s had been James Quinn, whose 'utterance is a continual sing-song, like the chanting of vespers,' the novelist Tobias Smollett complained through a character in his *Peregrine Pickle*. However, Quinn had great success in parts that called for declamation.

A reaction set in with the appearance of Charles Macklin, who transformed the part of Shylock from comedy to realism, evoking a famous tribute from Alexander Pope. 'This is the Jew, that Shakespeare drew,' he proclaimed. The Low Comedian had taken the part in Restoration times.

Macklin's triumph happened in the year of Garrick's debut as Richard III, and his career was overshadowed by him. He was quarrelsome and jealous yet he was a brilliant teacher and an often generous man. It was he who first dressed as a Highland chieftain to play Macbeth: Garrick and other actors had played him with no attempt at visual authenticity.

Garrick's electrifying Richard was first seen at Goodman's Fields Theatre on 19 October 1741. Audiences were so used to 'gentlemen acting for their diversion' as Garrick's biographer Davies puts it, that the house was not full. 'Quinn was the popular player,' Davies tells us, 'but his manner of heaving up his words, and his laboured action, prevented his being a favourite Richard.' On came Garrick, fortified by Richard's first sardonic thunderbolt of a speech. Davies continues the heady story:

Mr. Garrick's easy and familiar, yet forcible style in speaking and acting, at first threw the critics into some hesitation concerning the novelty as well as the propriety of his manner. They had long been accustomed to an elevation of the voice, with a sudden mechanical depression of its tones, calculated to excite admiration, and entrap applause. To the just modulation of the words, and concurring expression of the features from genuine workings of nature, they had been strangers, at least for some time. But after he had gone through a variety of scenes, in which he gave evident proofs of consummate art, and perfect knowledge of character, their doubts were turned into surprise and astonishment, from which they relieved themselves by large and reiterated applause.

And so the triumphant evening wore on, complete with 'shouts of approbation' at key moments. A supreme career had begun.

Garrick became the greatest English actor of his day, famous far beyond England, most notably in France, where he also acted. He triumphed equally in tragedy and comedy, in Hamlet and Macbeth and Lear as well as Benedick and Jonson's Abel Drugger. He was a theatre reformer who banished audiences from the stage; who concealed stage lighting

Left: Reynolds' oil painting of a Portrait of Garrick Between Tragedy and Comedy.

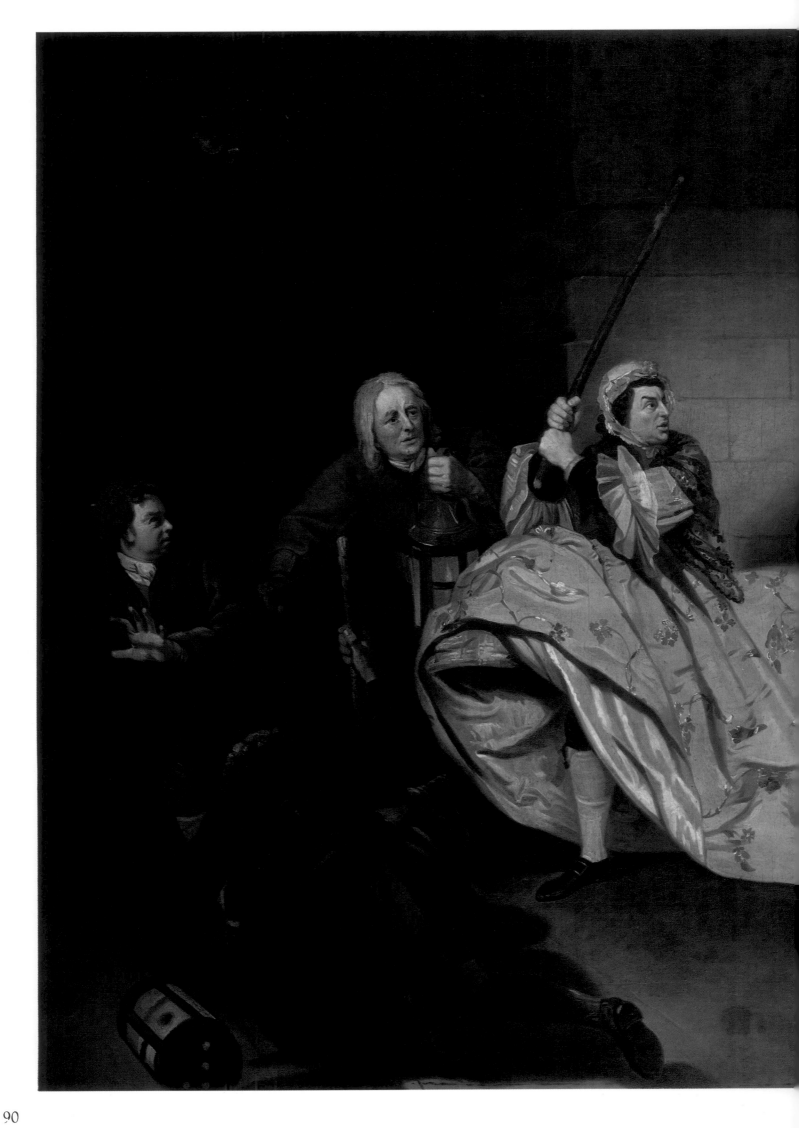

Left: David Garrick in female attire in Vanbrugh's The Provok'd Wife.

Right: The National
Theatre's revival of The
Rivals in 1983, with
Geraldine McEwen and
Michael Hordern, directed
by Peter Wood.

from the audience, and who used the great German designer and painter Phillipe de Loutherbourg from 1771 with maximum success. It was this Alsatian-born artist who brought the art of illusionist realistic scenery to the British stage.

Garrick saw to it that most of the leading actors of the day played with him at Drury Lane. He appears memorably in Henry Fielding's *Tom Jones*, the hero telling Mr. Partridge that most people consider that Garrick, whom they have just seen as Hamlet, is the best player in town:

He the best player! cries Partridge, with a contemptuous sneer. Why, I could act as well as he myself. I am sure, if I had seen a ghost, I should have looked in the very same

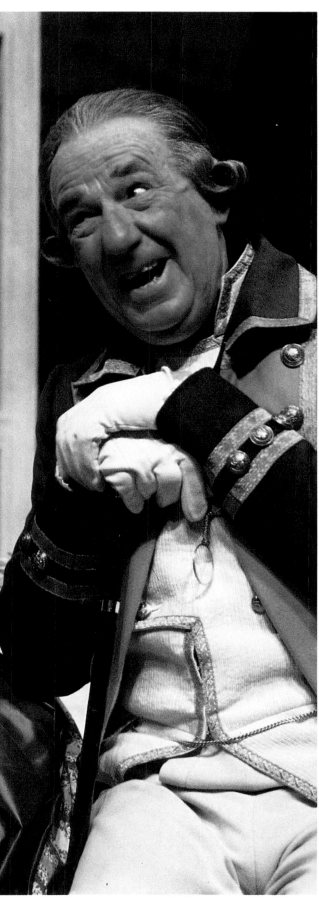

break the monopoly of Covent Garden and Drury Lane by getting permission to perform at the Haymarket during summer months when the two licensed theatres were closed.

The rest of the country was served with a growing number of theatres, but many acted wherever they could. John Bernard recalled the world of the strolling players in his book *Recollections of the Stage*. This was an age when companies literally took to the roads, though most at least had one wagon. It needed to be strong as the roads were often villainous. Permission was needed to act in a town, while trade had to be drummed up in the town centre. Bernard's first 'first night' took place in an inn. The manager had chosen a suitable room:

(He) suspended a collection of green tatters along its middle for a curtain, erected a pair of paper screens right-hand and left for wings; arranged four candles in front of said wings to divide the stage from the orchestra (the fiddlers' chairs being legitimate division of the orchestra from the Pit), and with all the spare benches of the inn to form boxes, and a hoop suspended from the ceiling (perforated with a dozen nails to receive as many tallow candles) to suggest the idea of a chandelier; he had constructed and embellished what denominated a theatre.

From an age of mainly forgotten plays those of Richard Brinsley Sheridan (1751–1816) are outstanding. An Anglo-Irishman, his career as a playwright was packed into the years 1775–9. *The Rivals* made his name, and the next year, 1776, he bought Garrick's share in Drury Lane

manner, and done just as he did . . . The king for my money! He speaks all his words, half as loud again as the other. Anyone may see he is an actor.

Garrick's leading ladies included Mrs Cibber, Mrs Bellamy and Peg Woffington. His triumphs inevitably led to jealousy, fanned by the evil wit of Samuel Foote. It was Foote who managed to

Below: The National Theatre's revival of Sheridan's The Critic, *Ian McKellen flanked by Jonathan Hyde (left) and Laurence Rudic.*

Right: A scene from Macbeth, *with John Philip Kemble as Macbeth and his sister Sarah Siddons as Lady Macbeth.*

Theatre, rebuilding it in 1794. His masterpiece, *The School for Scandal*, dates from 1777. Witty, funny, perfectly written and full of excellent parts, this classic high comedy has always been loved by actors and audiences.

Sheridan's other marvel is *The Critic* (1779), which starts as glorious high comedy and then becomes a play within a play, presented by the versatile Mr Puff.

Sheridan also presented a less bawdy version of Vanbrugh's *The Relapse* to suit the requirements of his day. It is good, but, as modern audiences know, the original is better.

His finest plays have been called High Georgian comedies, comedies of manners, and Restoration comedies without the licentiousness but with all their wit. Their prose is a glory, their sentimentality by no means overdone, while they are stocked with immortals: Mrs Malaprop,

Lady Teazle and many others. In an uncynical way his comedies mock human folly.

Alas, Sheridan himself had his share of folly as well as ill-fortune. Theatregoers can hardly hold his political career against him – he was one of the finest orators of his age – but having built his newer and larger Drury Lane in 1794, which seated over 3,600 people, too many for a theatre, he proceeded to neglect his company, many of whom deserted him for Covent Garden. Also, by concentrating on mammoth spectacles and pantomimes, he lost his best actors to Covent Garden and reduced Drury Lane to near bankruptcy. In February 1809, when he was speaking in the House of Commons, he heard that Drury Lane was in flames – theatre fires were common in those days – and left the House. He drank wine as he watched his theatre disintegrate. As his biographer

Thomas Moore wrote, 'on being encountered drinking a glass of wine in the street, said: "A man may surely be allowed to take a glass of wine by his own fireside."' A fourth Drury Lane was soon built. It is the theatre that we have today, though its auditorium is much altered.

The leading actress of the period was the redoubtable Sarah Siddons, arguably the greatest of English tragediennes. Born into a family of strolling players in 1755 as Sarah Kemble, after provincial successes she conquered London at her second attempt, creating a sensation as Isabella in Southern's play of that name at Drury Lane in 1782. The great Doctor Johnson called her a prodigious fine woman, and Gainsborough, Lawrence and Reynolds all painted her. Volumnia in *Coriolanus* and Lady Macbeth were two of her greatest roles. The great critic and essayist William Hazlitt proclaimed later: 'She was tragedy personified.' She virtually retired in 1812. Her younger brother, John Philip Kemble, who managed first Drury Lane and then Covent Garden, was a stately, graceful actor, overshadowed by the volcanic Edmund Kean, but he was a famous Coriolanus. His sister stole the show whenever she appeared as Volumnia, however. Charles Young recalled it in this classic tribute to grandeur:

I remember her coming down the stage in the triumphal entry of her son, Coriolanus, when her dumb-show drew plaudits that shook the building. She came alone, marching and beating time to the music; rolling (if that be not too strong a term to describe her motion) from side to side, swelling with the triumph of her son. Such was the intoxication of joy which flashed from her eye, and lit up her whole face, that the effect was irresistible. She seemed to me to reap all the glory of that procession to herself. I could not take my eye from her. Coriolanus, banner, pageant, all went for nothing to me, after she had walked to her place.

Left: Mrs Siddons rehearsing with her father Roger Kemble, by Thomas Rowlandson.

This engraving shows the first performance of Sheridan's masterpiece, A School for Scandal, *at Drury Lane Theatre on 8 May 1777.*

Right: The real Hans Sachs as opposed to Wagner's portrait of him in The Mastersingers.

Germany

'The first page of Shakespeare that I read made me aware that he and I were one . . . I had been as one born blind who first sees the light.' So wrote Johann Wolfgang von Goethe (1749–1832), man of letters, scientist, philosopher, statesman and genius. Yet long before this intoxicating moment the links between the English and German theatres had been formed.

It was not easy for Germany, split by wars, religious and secular, and without a capital city, to achieve a true theatrical identity. A development from the Mysteries had been the *Fastnachtsspiel*, a pre-Lenten carnival play, in which townspeople wandered round the town, performing in a number of places and mingling with the carnival crowds in between. These reached their height in Nuremberg in the late fifteenth and early sixteenth centuries, the master of the art being Hans Sachs, later immortalized by Wagner in *Die Meistersinger*. He wrote many morality plays, but it is carnival plays that made him a major theatrical figure.

A greater spur to the drama was given from the 1590s by troupes of English actors, who continued to visit Germany throughout the seventeenth century. The plays of Shakespeare and his colleagues and their successors were livened up considerably but Germany became truly theatre-conscious because of the English comedians.

By the late seventeenth century Italian spectacle was all the rage, with even the Latin Jesuit dramas performed by students finely mounted. However, this was drama for the few. In the early 1700s there was an attempt to create literary rather than the more popular drama, the improvised Harlequinades being much criticized by the reformers. Tediousness was the result, even if a plodding professionalism laid the foundations of serious theatre. French plays were studied, but the real revelation was Shakespeare. One reason his popularity

Left: Joseph Stephan's Wandering Comedians *in mid-eighteenth-century Germany.*

and prestige is so much higher in Germany than in France is that he has been blessed with more than one excellent German translator. He is now more performed than Schiller in the latter's homeland.

Perhaps it needed Johann Gottsched and his helper, the actress Carolina Neuber, to give the German theatre a sense of discipline and purpose, complete with a dose of French classics, for Gottsched aimed to reform the German theatre on French lines. He saw the theatre as a key part of a town, which is still so much a German concept. It took Britain two centuries to catch up with him, and even now his vision is not shared by a majority of Britons.

Germany's first great playwright was Gotthold Lessing (1729–81), who attacked Aristotle and the French classics and, not surprisingly, extolled Shakespeare. He was not averse to Greek drama as such and he dreamed of a theatre that combined Greek with Shakespearean drama. He even practised the unities of Aristotle. He also established bourgeois drama in Germany with his *Miss Sara Sampson*. His finest play is *Minna von Barnhelm* (1767), which heralded a new era in German comedy. Meanwhile, he never ceased championing the superiority of Shakespeare over the French in craftsmanship, characterisation and theatrical flair.

Italy

The Italian Carlo Goldoni, born in 1707, wrote over 200 plays, some in his native Venetian dialect, some in French. The Comédie-Italienne in Paris, though it performed in French in his day, attracted him, and he settled in the city in the 1760s.

He was a true reformer, aiming to substitute written plays for the now decadent *commedia dell'arte* ones. He also refused to contribute to the flow of mannered verse plays of the day. He aimed at the middle classes and criticized the aristocracy and his women's roles were better than his men's. *La Locandiera* (1751) is one of his best plays and later gave Eleanore Duse a favourite role.

Carlo Gozzi (1720–1806), unlike Goldoni, tried to reform *commedia dell'arte* by turning it into written theatre. A witty writer, even in his own day he was considered an extravagant one. He created what he called a *fiaba*, mixing

fantasy and comedy, but today he is best remembered as the inspiration for two operas, Puccini's *Turandot* and Prokofiev's *The Love of Three Oranges*. His memoirs make marvellous reading.

The third Italian playwright of the period was Vittorio Alfieri (1749–1803), who wrote classical verse tragedies, featuring superhuman characters from history, the Bible and myth. His tragedies are not forgotten, notably *Oreste*, which was revived for his bicentenary with Vittorio Gassmann in the lead, directed by Visconti.

In fact, Italian drama was already overshadowed by the runaway popularity of opera, even though few of those eighteenth-century operas are now performed, even in Italy. Opera buffa – comic opera – was all the rage and the plays of Goldoni were happily plundered by librettists. Naples was the centre of

Left: A ball at the great San Carlo Opera House in Naples.

opera buffa, in which the everyday life of the people exploded onto the stage. However, it was Rossini, born in 1792, who conquered the world, to be followed by other immortals. If conquered seems too strong a word, one must cite Stendhal, who started Rossini's biography by announcing that Napoleon was dead, but that a new conqueror had appeared whose name was on every lip from Moscow to Naples, from London to Vienna, from Paris to Calcutta (sic.). Poor Gozzi and Goldoni never got that sort of treatment.

The Americas

The theatre reached the Americas early in the sixteenth century with religious plays brought by the Spaniards. Masques were performed in French Canada early in the following century, by which time there were professional Spanish actors in the New World.

The Puritans held sway in New England. That scourge of sin, Increase Mather, was appalled to hear in 1687 that 'Stage-Plays' were about to be performed, but any perfomances that did take place must have been staged in private houses. In 1750, the over-godly in Massachusetts heard with horror that British officers were putting on plays from time to time, even charging money for them to eke out their pay. The province promptly banned such diversions.

Happily, the colonies in the South were far from biased against the stage. Williamsburg, Virginia, had a playhouse from around 1716. Charles-Town, as it then was, in South Carolina, was a theatre centre by the mid-eighteenth century, having enjoyed putting on many plays since 1703.

BOSTON THEATRE.

THE BATTLE OF BUNKER HILL, FOR THIS NIGHT ONLY.

The Grand Washington Transparency, for the fourth time.........Tekeli, for the last time this season.

THIS EVENING, (WEDNESDAY,) APRIL 5th, 1820,

Will be performed, (first and only, time for several years,) the Patriotic Play, in 5 acts, called the

Battle of Bunker Hill.

"*Let the Rallying Word through all the Day, be,* LIBERTY OR DEATH,"

Of Rome's and Cato's fall, the World has rung:
Why not Columbia's rising fame be sung?
If Rome her Brutus, and her Cato boast,
Her Washington, and Warren, each a host,
Columbia owns ; with thousand names beside,
The least of which, would swell the Roman Pride.

Gen. Warren, - - - - - Mr. Pelby.	Sir William Howe, - - - - - Mr. Holland.
Gen. Prescott, - - - - - Mr. Adamson.	Gen. Gage, - - - - - Mr. McCulley.
Gen. Putnam, - - - - - Mr. Dykes.	Harman, - - - - - Mr. Baker.
Abercrombie, - - - - - Mr. Williams.	American Soldier, - - - - - Mr. Spooner.
Elvira, - - - - - Mrs. Young.	Anna, - - - - - Miss Jones.

ACT FIRST........SCENE FIRST.

A VIEW OF STATE STREET..............LORD PERCY AND BRITISH SOLDIERS,

Returning, fatigued and disordered, from Lexington....................Act Second, CHAMBER....GENERAL WARREN
discovered *Reading a Letter*, which announces the DEFEAT AT LEXINGTON...........Act Third,

*A View of the American Camp.....*Act Fourth, *A View of Bunker Hill....*Bunker Hill Fortified.

THE BATTLE....CHARLESTOWN IN FLAMES !

The BRITISH march towards the Hill, to the Music of "*Yankee Doodle*"....Three times they make the Assault, and each time are
driven back....After the third Repulse, WARREN descends and Addresses the AMERICANS....The BATTLE is renewed, GEN-
ERAL WARREN *receives a Mortal Wound, and Dies for his Country !*

End of the Play, an Interlude, (fourth time,) in which will be Displayed, A GRAND HISTORICAL and EMBLEMATICAL

TRANSPARENCY.

DELINEATING the IMPORTANT EVENTS in the MILITARY and CIVIL LIFE of the ILLUSTRIOUS WASHINGTON.

IN THE BACK OF WHICH, IS

a Whole Length Figure of WASHINGTON ; at his feet, Civil and Military Emblems ; and on each side, the Ensigns of his Country......On the Cornice of the Pedestal, is inscribed : "*Born February 22d, 1732 ;*"......On the Plinth : "*Died December 13th, 1799.*"

IN THE CENTRE OF THE FRIZE, AND SUPPORTED BY THE COLUMNS, IS A KEY STONE, ON WHICH IS WRITTEN :

"*First in War, First in Peace, and First in the Hearts of His Fellow Citizens.*"............Under, in the Horizon, are the *Thirteen
Stars,* Emblematic of the *Thirteen Original States.*

The Standard of Liberty ! Addressed to the Armies of the United States, - - - *by Mrs. Williams.*

To which will be added, (last time this season,) the Grand Melo Drama, in 3 acts, called

TEKELI.

Count Tekeli, Mr. Williams.	Edmund, - - - Mr. Baker.	Conrad, - - - Mr. Pelby.
Wolf, *(his friend,)* - Mr. Charnock.	Frank, - - - Mr. Holland.	Maurice, - - - Mr. Adamson.
Brasdefer, - Mr. Bray.	Count Caraffa, - Mr. McCulley.	Isidore, - - - Mr. Jones.
Alexina, - Mrs. Powell.	Christine, - Miss Jones.	Officer, - - - Mr. Spooner.

Due notice will be given of the second performance of *Raymond and Agnes*...Also, of the fourth representation of *Cinderella.*

TIME OF RISING THE CURTAIN IS ALTERED TO QUARTER BEFORE SEVEN O'CLOCK.

Right: Nineteenth century audiences expected their money's worth.

The Quakers of Pennsylvania banned plays, but a playhouse was built just outside Philadelphia's town limits. Plays were billed as moral spectacles, dialogues or lectures in tricky areas. Newport, Rhode Island, staged a performance of *Othello* in 1761, advertised as 'Moral Dialogues in Five Parts, Depicting the evil effects of jealousy ... and proving that happiness can only spring from the pursuit of virtue.'

By now New York, too, was on the theatrical map, with two theatres by the 1750s. During the Revolution the city was in British and Loyalist hands for most of the war until the peace of 1783. British officers acted at the John Street Theatre, forming the Garrison Dramatic Club, and George Washington saw Addison's *Cato* when he and his army were enduring a winter at Valley Forge.

The old suspicion of theatre broke out once more in some places after the war. It was feared that passions might be too aroused. There was no stopping it now, however. The first American comedy, *The Contrast*, by Royall Tyler, was produced in New York in 1787. In 1794 the Chestnut Theatre, a replica of the Theatre Royal in Bath, was opened in Philadelphia (the capital city). It was probably America's first gaslit theatre (1816). As for that dedicated theatregoer and playreader, George Washington, one of his very favourite plays was *The School for Scandal*. Soon the way west would carry theatre and entertainment generally all over the fast-growing new nation.

ROMANTICS
by Gaslight

The late eighteenth and early nineteenth centuries were hugely exciting in theatre history, even if great new plays were in short supply. The Romantic era affected all the arts, though the word 'romantic' does not indicate that previous generations did not write, paint, compose or act romantically. Is the more formal Mozart less 'romantic' than Beethoven, Beethoven than Berlioz? No, but the Romantics exploited their feelings about their subjects more passionately, emotionally and subjectively, and were not so concerned with form and 'reality'. Actors and actresses, too, were affected, Kean and a host of others. The players were the kings and queens of this era, Shakespeare and often one-dimensional melodramas being popular fare. The 'well-made' plays, which will be noted, did not kill off the more lusty melodramas until our century, while well-made plays, good and trivial, will always be with us.

Germany

Romantic Theatre was born in Germany, to which we must now return, also to Goethe. Believing that in the drama of the future the Greeks' conception of tragic fate must be allied to the Shakespearean vision of tragic will, he was one of the *Sturm und Drang* – Storm and Stress – school of playwrights, the name taken from a play by Klinger. Shakespeare was the school's particular idol, and Goethe's *Götz von Berlichingen* of 1773 was such a play. This 'action-packed portrait of a robber baron' was followed by the historical play *Egmont*, best known outside Germany for its incidental music by Beethoven. It followed very closely his influential *Die Leiden des jungen Werthers* (The Sorrows of Young Werther), which

is said to have sent the suicide rate up in Germany, victims following Werther himself to the grave. His *Faust*, written in two parts over many years, is too vast a conception to be judged as a conventional play. It is a *Gesamtkunstwerk*, a mixture of drama, poetry, music, song and the visual arts into a complete work of art. Wagner is the other great name associated with the concept. In fact, it has influenced literature more than the theatre.

Above: The German theatre was fortunate that Goethe was so dedicated to the theatre. With Schiller's help he made it a very influential artistic centre.

Above: The National Theatre's 1982 production of The Prince of Homburg *by Heinrich von Kleist, which asks if self-mastery is actually self-denial. Left to right: Robert Urquhart, Mary Macleod, Lindsay Duncan and Patrick Drury.*

Goethe also managed the Weimar Theatre with Freidrich von Schiller for a time. Schiller (1759–1805), best known outside the German-speaking world for the operas based on his plays (including Rossini's *William Tell* and Verdi's *Don Carlo*), made his name in 1781 when, at Mannheim, *Die Rauber* (The Robbers) created a sensation. Total strangers embraced each other in floods of tears, and people fainted as they headed for the exits. This was catharsis! Schiller's plays were long, *Don Carlos* almost twice the length of *Hamlet*. However, his plays were enormously popular throughout the nineteenth century in Germany and eas-

tern Europe, second only to Shakespeare's.

In fact, Germany, as elsewhere, was now to suffer a period when all-too-often fine acting was put to the service of poor plays. August von Kotzebue (1761–1819) wrote melodramas and sentimental comedies, but the important playwright, Heinrich von Kleist (1777–1811) was reduced to suicide, not knowing that one day his *Der zerbrochene Krug* (The Broken Jug) and *Prinz Friedrich von Homburg*, a heroic tragedy, would be much admired. The second explores his eternal problem–whether self-mastery is also self-denial.

sheerest melodrama when spoken by merely good actors:

> Ha! I am feeble:
> Some undone widow sits upon mine arm,
> And takes away the use of it; and my sword,
> Glued to my scabbard with wrong'd
>   orphans' tears
> Will not be drawn . . .

It was an age of gaslight as well as melodrama, gas being installed in Drury Lane in 1817.

Edmund Kean's battleground-in-chief was Drury Lane. It was there that on a famous night in 1814 he entered as Shylock to face a half-filled auditorium and made himself a theatre immortal.

Kean had nothing in his favour but his striking eyes and his genius, yet Leigh Hunt was to describe his 'exceeding grace, his gallant levity, his measureless dignity; for his little person absolutely becomes tall'. His fame was such that Dumas père wrote a play about him. His scandalous personal life was a gift to the newspapers

Below: Edmund Kean as Sir Giles Overreach in A New Way to Pay Old Debts, *a role in which he sent Lord Byron into a convulsion.*

England

The early nineteenth century was short on dramatic invention, yet the theatre itself flourished on both sides of the Atlantic, in the young United States especially in Philadelphia. The greatest stars crossed to act in America, including Edmund Kean and Rachel, perhaps the greatest of French tragediennes.

On 12 January 1816, at Drury Lane Theatre, Lord Byron was sent into a convulsion by Kean and a number of ladies fainted. The play, *A New Way to Pay Old Debts*, was by the Jacobean dramatist Massinger. His villain, Sir Giles Overreach, uttered lines that would be

MR KEAN AS RICHARD THE THIRD.
Act V. Scene Last.

Glos. Perdition catch thy Arm   the chance is thine
But Oh! the vast Renown thou hast acquired
In conquering Richard does afflict him more
Than even his Body's parting with its Soul
Now let the World no longer be a stage

To feed contention in a lingering Act
But let one Spirit of the first born Cain
Reign in all Bosoms that each Heart being set
On bloody actions the rude Scene may end
And darkness be the burier of the dead   Dies

The Original Sketch in the possession of Rob.t Albion Cox Esq.r

*Above: The Great
Edmund Kean as Richard
III. Like many others he
was even finer as Iago.*

of the day. Born in 1789, and, possibly, the most thrilling of all English actors, he died of drink at the height of his powers in 1833. Richard III, Iago and Othello were three of his most famous roles. He was not one to allow other actors near him and even warm admirers like William Hazlitt were prepared to criticize some of his methods and mannerisms. Yet he remains the actor of the past that most theatregoers with a love of stage history would give fortunes to have seen. The poet Coleridge said that to see him 'was to read Shakespeare by flashes of lightning'. Leigh Hunt compared Kean to John Kemble in a long essay.

The distinction between Kean and Kemble may be briefly stated to be this: that Kemble knew there was a difference between tragedy and common life, but did not know in what it consisted, except in *manner*, which he consequently carried to excess, losing sight of the passion. Kean knows the real thing, which is the height of the *passion*, manner following it as a matter of course, and grace being developed from it in proportion to the truth of the sensation . . .

Later in the essay Leigh Hunt, having made the modern reader rather sorry for the handsome Kemble's clear inability to move his audience, although to impress them, sums up Kean as only a magnificent and perceptive writer could:

Now Kean we never see without being moved, and moved too in fifty ways – by his sarcasm, his sweetness, his pathos, his exceeding grace, his gallant levity, his measureless dignity: for his little person absolutely becomes tall, and rises to the height of moral grandeur, in such characters as Othello. We have seen him with three or four persons round him, all taller than he, but himself so graceful, so tranquil, so superior, so nobly possessed, in the midst, that the mind of the spectator rose above them by his means, and so gave him a moral stature that confounded itself with the personal.

It was a great age of pantomime, that 'Traditional Christmas entertainments of the British Empire', as old editions of the *Oxford Companion to the Theatre* call it. Beginning in the eighteenth century, it stemmed from the *commedia dell'arte* and the harlequinade, which was a feature of British pantomime until this century. Harlequin, Pantaloon and Columbine starred in a madcap blend of music, magic and mime. Occasionally, they have been seen in modern pantomimes, which have nothing to do as a rule with mime.

In the early nineteenth century pantomime was a magical affair. The superstar was an Anglo-Italian, Joseph Grimaldi, born in 1778, who ruled Covent Garden for many years. He was actor, dancer, singer, mime and the greatest British theatre clown. He was not

Below: The harlequinade, for many years a feature in British pantomimes.

MR. J. S. GRIMALDI.

(as Scaramouch.)

106

a circus performer, but clowns in the British circuses have always been called Joeys in his honour. He died in 1837, widely mourned.

Pantomime reached its strange and wondrous modern form in the mid-nineteenth century. Topical gags abound and audiences participate from time to time. The Dame, a key comic character, is played by a man. Blue jokes are not welcomed by traditionalists, but a transformation scene is.

The form still survives, even though there are now men playing Principal Boys, a major break with tradition. It can embrace everything from a fairy tale – Cinderella is the most popular – complete with magic – to pop, acrobats and a bicycle act.

Melodramas were hugely popular throughout the nineteenth century, two of them living on in theatre legend and occasionally in performance – *Maria Marten* and *Sweeney Todd*. Melodramas had a bonus beyond entertaining enormous audiences, for they also brought out the best in machinists and carpenters. Dogs and horses performed

on stage throughout theatrical Europe. At the end of the century *Ben Hur*, complete with chariot race, was presented in New York. Audiences enjoyed these marvels all the more because gas lighting improved on candlelight and was also controllable; then, in the 1880s, electric lighting improved on gas.

The British theatre went into a long decline in the 1820s. Audiences got rougher, so the middle classes deserted the theatre, all but the hard core of theatre-lovers. William Macready, a great or near great actor, had the misfortune to be acting in this period. He was one of the first to return to Shakespeare's texts, abandoning the 'improvements' that had survived for so long, though gradually diminishing down the years. He was a very fine Lear, Hamlet and Macbeth and he tried to bring famous writers into the theatre, only succeeding with Bulwer Lytton's *Richelieu* and *The Lady of Lyons*. Finally, he left the stage in 1851. His frank, rather pompous *Journal* makes marvellous reading, but also reveals how often he disliked and how sometimes he hated his profession.

Above: Audiences expected and got scenic marvels in the last century, like this horse race in Paris. Trains on stage were also popular stunts.

Opposite: Grimaldi, greatest of British clowns, as Scaramouch.

107

France

In France Romanticism had moments of heady glory when the staid Comédie-Française allowed Victor Hugo's *Hernani* on to its revered stage on 25 February 1830. A splendid uproar, then a battle, took place, with classical enthusiasts enraged by Hugo's often – for them – overfree methods. The old brigade roared: 'Racine! Racine!' but their juniors and more enlightened contemporaries shouted their support for the new man. Then came a famous moment: Théophile Gautier, poet, novelist and critic, rose to his feet and called: 'Your Racine is a scamp, gentlemen!' Hugo's later *Le Roi s'amuse* was banned in 1832 after a single performance. It is best remembered in its operatic version, *Rigoletto*, in which Verdi made the king a duke, as the authorities were uneasy about a licentious king being on stage.

These were heady times for Romantics. Hector Berlioz, for many France's greatest composer, was one. He was one of a minority in France who appreciated Shakespeare after seeing Charles Kemble's company in Paris. He fell in love with the Ophelia, Harriet Smithson, who became his wife. It was an unhappy marriage, but she and – through her – Shakespeare triumphed with the Romantics, making far more mark than she had in London. She revealed Shakespeare to France, so one critic declared, after seeing her Desdemona opposite Macready's Othello.

Dumas père was another Romantic playwright, and his son, also Alexandre, wrote the famous *La Dame aux Camélias* (Lady of the Camellias), later turned into an even more famous opera by Verdi. Unhappy about his upbringing and illegitimacy, he later wrote plays on moral issues.

Romanticism did not last long in France, but melodramas thrived. One of the leading actors was Frédérick Lemaître, whose repertoire included Hamlet and Othello and the plays of Dumas père. Because of *Les Enfants du Paradis*, that magical film recreation of the Romantic period in Paris, he will, also thanks to Pierre Brasseur's performance, never be forgotten, and nor will the incomparable mime Deburau, portrayed by the great Jean-Louis Barrault.

Other French playwrights included Eugene Labiche (1815–88), who wrote more than 150 plays and was France's leading comic dramatist. His *Un Chapeau de paille d'Italie* (An Italian Straw Hat) is well known outside France. He scourged the middle classes in his comedies and farces and they adored him. His contemporary Emile Augier believed in bourgeois ideals, writing comedies of manners and – in *Le Mariage d'Olympe* – creating a very different courtesan from Dumas's *Lady of the Camellias*. Alfred de Musset wrote a number of plays for reading, but *Fantasio* and *Lorenzaccio* were successfully staged. They are bitter-sweet comedies, extravagant and romantic. He died in 1857. The other gifted playwright of the period was Alfred de Vigny, whose *Chatterton* (1835) inspired his fellow Romantics. A poet as well as a playwright, he extolled William Shakespeare at the expense of Racine, adapting some of his plays.

During this period Eugene Scribe (1791–1861) created the later much abused 'well-made play', lacking true characterization and psychology. He produced some 400 featherweight vaudevilles complete with musical intervals, provided many opera libretti, some of them very good, and 35 plays, including the famous tragedy, *Adrienne Lecouvreur* with Ernest Legouvé. The well-made play at its best is admirable, however much it has been abused.

The greatest tragedienne of her day, Rachel (1820–58) scored a triumph in *Adrienne Lecouvreur*. She was a poor Jewish street singer who became the greatest, perhaps, of all French tragediennes. Joining the Comédie-Française in 1838, she excelled as Phèdre and other great roles, touring widely, including America in 1855. She died of consumption and overwork in her thirties. Her intensity and power have assured that she will never be forgotten.

Below: A scene from Verdi's La Traviata, *with June Anderson as Violetta, a Welsh National Opera production.*

Opposite: Marie Taglioni, the queen of ballet's Romantic era.

Right: Peter Finch and John Phillips in Labiche's An Italian Straw Hat *at the Old Vic in 1952.*

Below: Rachel as Phèdre. *A poor Jewish girl, she became a great tragedienne, dying in her thirties of overwork and consumption.*

It was an age of rocket-like rises to fame by women of genius. There was the incomparable actress-singer Marie Malibran, who inspired Bellini and so overwhelmed the stern Duke of Wellington that he held her hand for almost ten minutes and nearly broke it. She died in 1836, aged only 28. There was also the Italian dancer Marie Taglioni, whose *La Sylphide* (1832) marked the birth of Romantic ballet, and Carlotta Grisi, the first Giselle (1841).

In the midst of this splendid welter of Romanticism, a German dramatist and poet appeared whose influence was to be colossal even though he died at the age of 23, having written only three plays, one of them unfinished. This was George Büchner (1813–37), who reacted against the romantic extremes of Schiller and others and anticipated not only the more natural drama that came in half a century after his death, but also the Expressionists. His plays are full of violence, of morbid psychological insight. They are *Danton's Death* (1835), *Leonce and Lena* (1836) and *Woyzeck* (1836), the last unfinished, and the inspiration of Berg's opera. *Danton* is about the great Revolutionary Frenchman and reflects the playwright's pessimism and passionate love of freedom.

Other European countries' native playwrights of great merit, included the Czech Josef Tyl, who ranged widely and

Right: Büchner's *Danton's Death at the National Theatre in 1971. Left to right: Ronald Pickup, Charles Kay and Christopher Plummer as Danton.*

Below: The English National Opera's Orpheus in the Underworld, *with striking sets and costumes by Gerald Scarfe.*

in one play portrayed miners on stage. Juliusz Slowacki of Poland wrote historical dramas and comedies, and another Pole, Zygmunt Krasinski wrote a Romantic masterpiece, *Nieboska Komedia* in 1833, though it was not staged until 1902.

Operas and operettas

Though his field was opera, Richard Wagner (1813–83) was a very influential figure. His vision of the total work of art, the *Gesamtkunstwerk*, was only truly achieved after the Second World War at Bayreuth by his grandchildren, Wieland and Wolfgang. The first Bayreuth Festival was in 1876, but Wagner never saw his theatrical ideals achieved. It was all he could do, even with the help of King Ludwig of Bavaria, to reach high musical standards, and he had to make do with commonplace designs in an age when design was not inspired. Yet the theatre was brilliantly conceived and Wagner holds a brave place in the history of theatre as well as opera.

Italian opera, which reached its peak in the long career of Verdi (1813–1901) provides a rare example of great *new* art being truly popular with all classes – as happened in Shakespeare's day in England. Verdi's career stretches from *Oberto* (1839) to *Falstaff* (1893). In a lighter vein the operettas of the Strauss family enraptured Vienna and audiences far beyond it. Johann Strauss II was the king of operetta in Germany and Austria, and, later, Franz Léhar, composer of *The Merry Widow*. A German Jew who settled in France and changed his name to Jacques Offenbach was the operetta king of Paris. Musically, he was the king of the genre. Rossini dubbed him the Mozart of the Champs-Elysées and meant it; Wagner noted that he had the savoir faire of the divine Mozart. His satire, topical and strong, is mainly lost on us today, but his best operettas – *Orpheus in the Underworld*, *La Belle Hélène* and a handful of others are exhilarating, enchanting and timeless. He fell from grace after France was defeated in the Franco-Prussian war of 1870, being associated with the defeated régime (which he had anyway mocked). He is the personification of comic and melodic musical theatre.

Britain's chief contribution to the enjoyable genre are, of course, the Savoy Operas of Gilbert and Sullivan. William Schenck Gilbert (1836–1911) and (later

Sir) Arthur Sullivan (1842–1900) were hardly the happiest of partners and, indeed, famously split up for a time, but their partnership resulted in 13 light operas, most of which were colossal successes in Britain and America. They remain much loved. Gilbert also wrote burlesques and fantasies and a number of plays, but the works that matter are *The*

Above: Richard Wagner was the most controversial musical genius of the nineteenth century and a major theatrical figure. His grandchildren Wieland and Wolfgang finally fulfilled his vision of true music dramas.

Mikado, The Gondoliers, The Pirates of Penzance, Iolanthe and the rest, most of which had their premières at the Savoy. The pair had a brilliant manager in Richard D'Oyly Carte. Their first success was *Trial By Jury* in 1875. Gilbert was a brilliant producer (as directors were called in Britain until the 1960s) and one of the first of the breed. Directing in Victorian and Edwardian times was normally done by the leading actor/actor-manager. In his day the newly minted productions were clearly first-rate, but the D'Oyly Carte Company never changed Gilbert's original stage directions and minor works of art became not unenjoyable museum pieces. Until the copyrights on the music and words expired the D'Oyly Carte Company also prevented other professional companies staging the works in Britain.

Germany on tour

Meanwhile, the Duke of Saxe-Meiningen had been doing for the German – and European – theatre what Wagner and his patron King Ludwig had been doing for opera. He founded a troupe, the Meiningers, in 1874. His wife was a niece of Queen Victoria and during visits to England the Duke became interested in the work of Edmund Kean's son Charles at the Princess Theatre. A competent actor, Kean's detailed staging, his crowd scenes, made up for his lack of true theatrical genius. The Duke and his assistant, Ludwig Chronegk, went even further than Kean. Every member of the crowds was a character, while the crowd itself was divided into groups, each with its own leader. The centre of the stage picture never coincided with the centre of the stage, and continuous action was encouraged by different levels provided by steps and rostra. A student of history and art, the Duke demanded detailed costumes, décor and scenery, interiors being box sets.

Every actor had his place, indeed no actor was recruited while the company was on tour: he or she would not fit into the ensemble. Even walk-on parts could hope to become important actors. The company toured until 1890 and influenced theatrical Europe. Stanislavsky and the Moscow Art Theatre, also the French director André Antoine, a great and pioneering director in the late nineteenth century, were among the many to be inspired by the Duke and his

MR C. KEAN AS GLOSTER.
RICHARD III.
GLO: Now is the winter of our discontent
Made glorious summer by this sun of York.
Act 1, Sc 1.

troupe. Antoine took over the Theatre Libre in 1887 to stage the work of new naturalistic playwrights, both French and foreign. In its nine years of existence it staged 184 plays, including those of Strindberg and Ibsen.

Back to England

Sir Henry Irving (1838–1905) was quick to realize what could be learnt from the Meiningers when he saw them at Drury Lane in 1881 playing Shakespeare. Shortly after his death the cult of underplaying assailed the British theatre and Irving and his methods were regarded, especially by those who had never seen him act, as ham. (This rude term refers to actors who overdo things

Above: Poor Charles Kean lived in the shadow of his mighty father, yet he had a fine career. He used too much elaborate scenery but handled crowds superbly in his role as actor-manager.

Opposite: Trade cards designed in 1885 to celebrate the first production of The Mikado.

or those whose technique is crude. Between the world wars it was even used about good actors who acted with any passion, as opposed to underplayed. The term is thought to stem from 'ham fatter', an American phrase, ham fat being used by raw country actors in past times as a make-up base for removing make-up.)

Irving was important for two reasons, for his tremendous powers as an actor and for the influence he had on the English stage as a whole, though he did little for new drama when it resurfaced after a bleak period. Samuel Phelps (1804–78), a Shakespearean who ran old Sadler's Wells Theatre from 1843–62, giving nearly all the plays in 4,000 performances over 18 years, was an admirable figure. So was Tom Robertson (1829–71), whose plays, especially *Caste* (1867), introduced realism into an era of melodramatic and romantic excess. He was also concerned with 'real' settings, props and sensible plots though they seem artificial now. He was later immortalized by Pinero as Tom Wrench in *Trelawny of the Wells*.

Meanwhile, the Somerset-born Irving, abandoning his counting house job in London, made his first professional appearance at the Lyceum, Sunderland, in 1856. A local critic advised him to take the first steamship home. In Edinburgh he stayed two years and acted 429 parts in 782 days – at a time when many companies had a huge repertoire of plays, often giving two in an evening, and a young actor would be expected to play several parts in some of them. His first London success came in 1866 in *The Belle's Stratagem*, but theatre immortality came to him on the first night of *The Bells* in 1871, a good melodrama in which he played the guilt-ridden burgomaster Matthias. Three years later his Hamlet – gentle, tender and therefore controversial at that time – established him as the leader of his profession.

In 1878 Irving acquired the Lyceum Theatre and built up a staff of over 600. Tennyson and Bulwer Lytton wrote plays for him and Burne Jones was one of his designers. The brilliant and adored Ellen Terry often acted with him. He was

Below: The old Sadler's Wells Theatre which opened in 1765. Between 1844 and 1862 Samuel Phelps produced 34 of Shakespeare's plays there.

Left: Sir Henry Irving as Cardinal Wolsey in Henry VIII.

criticized by a strenuous minority for mannerisms of speech and movement and attacked for his lack of enthusiasm for new plays, provoking often foolish attacks by the young Bernard Shaw. Yet he built up a fine company, training his actors superbly. His most acclaimed roles included Shylock, Thomas a'Becket in Tennyson's play, and Macbeth, in which Ellen Terry said that he was like a famished wolf. He gave the theatre the blackout for changing scenery, he presented elaborate productions, and, more than anyone else, brought the middle classes back to the theatre. He concerned himself with lighting and décor, indeed everything that concerned the theatre, and if his choice of plays was limited it was because for most of his career there was precious little to act in except for Shakespeare and melodramas.

Irving held his audiences in his thrall, and his power to startle and surprise made him constantly fascinating. On occasion he achieved greatness. Having made several fortunes, he died penniless. He had just completed a performance of *Becket* at Bradford with the words 'Into thye hands, O Lord, into thy hands'. He was the first actor to be knighted and, like Garrick, he was buried among kings and queens in Westminster Abbey, having started life humbly as Henry Brodribb.

Irving had lived in the great age of touring: he toured the United States eight times, usually visiting Canada as well. Touring flourished until the cinema started eroding theatre audiences, a process that television would continue until now it survives only on a modest scale. Today's tours are either pre- or post-London, or New York ones, with occasional tours in their own right. Yet at the turn of the century in Britain alone there were several hundred such tours 'on the road' at any given time, some grand No. 1 tours, less grand No. 2s, others modest No. 3s. Provincial cities and towns could hold them all: there was no shortage of theatres. And some actors made very good livings without ever coming to London – or New York. Frederick Victor, who occasionally appeared in London in the first half of this century, toured a Napoleonic play called *A Royal Divorce* in Edwardian times for most of every year for seven years, with a new horse every Monday!

Every theatrical nation had similar touring companies, whatever the regional differences, and many had stock companies like that which Dickens immortalized in *Nicholas Nickleby*. These (just) survived the Second World War. Each actor and actress had their category which affected the parts they played in *Hamlet*, *Maria Marten* or whatever. The tragedian naturally played Hamlet, the heavy woman Lady Macbeth, the low comedian the broad and farcical parts, and so on.

America

Touring in Britain, rugged as it was, was and is a modest affair compared with touring in the vast United States, especially before the continent was finally spanned by rail in 1869. 'Romantic' it seems when read about, but in real life it was gruelling until a network of rails criss-crossed the nation.

In gold-rush California every sort of entertainment flourished, most notably in San Francisco. In the 1850s some 907 plays were staged there, also 84 extravaganzas, pantomimes and ballets, 48 operas and 66 minstrel shows. Sacramento had its first theatre in 1849, San Francisco in 1850. Wandering minstrels and entertainers were welcome, but actresses, any actresses, even more so,

Below: Train Call! There were hundreds of shows 'on the road' until first the cinema and then television eroded the touring circuit. Old friends often met on Sundays at Crewe, where everyone seemed to change trains!

such was the shortage of women. Actors, unless competent, were likely to attract the bird, or vegetables.

Edwin Booth, whose fabulous career is discussed later, played in California in the early 1850s, giving the miners his Lear, Shylock etc., but the greatest attraction was the Irish-born Lola Montez. Her spider dance – she fought them off – and other acts were unremarkable, but her person made up for that. She taught a miner's daughter, Lola Crabtree, who later became a great comedienne.

Child stars were much admired, nine-year-old Ellen Bateman – who later acted with Irving – giving the miners her Hamlet and Richard III! The miners had a hard life and inevitably they wanted comedy – in plays, minstrel shows and entertainment generally. Serious offerings had to be very well performed.

Ironically and sadly, the first great American actor had to make his name in Europe as he was black. This was Ira Aldridge (1804–67), who may have been Edmund Kean's servant when the great

Above: Ira Aldridge, the great actor who may never have acted in his native America. He made his London début as Othello and played Lear in Russia.

121

English actor first toured the United States in 1820. He returned with Kean and made his London debut in 1826, billed as 'The African Roscius', playing Othello. In Ireland his Iago was Charles Kean. He acted widely in Europe, Russia included, with his greatest successes in Germany. He may have acted once in America – in Baltimore in the 1830s – but, assuming that he did, had little success. Lear was one of his most famous roles. He died in Poland in 1867.

A number of English stars were imported to act in America, the first of which was George Frederick Cooke, who gave some of his most celebrated roles in New York in 1810: Shylock, Sir Giles Overreach and Richard III. Edmund Kean, Macready and others followed. The first great American tragedian was Edwin Forrest (1806–72), 'a vast animal' but 'bewildered by a grain of genius' according to one writer, William Winter. He looked and sounded powerful, and once he had cured himself of ranting, he became a splendid Shakespearean. He succeeded in London in 1836, but nine years later had a hostile reception, blaming Macready for it. The long-term result of the bitter rivalry between Macready and Forrest was the notorious

Astor Place riot in New York in 1849, a bloody affray that left 22 dead and 36 wounded from the rifles of the militia.

Forrest disrupted his rival's performance one night as at previous performances, bringing it to a standstill, but, as John Coleman reported, when Forrest had retreated, 'Then Macready, like a man possessed, leaped into the breach, and took the house by storm. Surely he must have been inspired by the ordeal through which he had passed. Such a delirium of excitement for actors and audience as followed that Play scene and the Closet scene I have rarely, if ever, witnessed.' And when it was over rioting outside reached heights of starkest tragedy. The critic Howard Taubman wrote in his *The Making of the American Theatre* in 1965:

Succeeding generations of Americans have been stirred to frantic exhibitions of anger and adulation, but not even the Frank Sinatras, Johnny Rays, Elvis Presleys and the Beatles have got the public that whipped up.

Forrest was a magnificent bull of a man, but the poet Walt Whitman, writing in the *Brooklyn Eagle* in 1846 about his Spartacus, was worried about the effect he might have on younger actors. He felt that 'vapid imitators may spread quite all the faults of that style, with none of its excellencies ... We allude to the loud-mouthed ranting style – the tearing of everything to tatters.'

Whitman also complained of the critics who were 'the slaves of the paid puff system', and proclaimed that English plays, actors and managers 'must be allowed to die away among us, as usurpers of our stage'. He wanted, of course, an *American* theatre, but it was foolish to suggest discarding the chance of seeing what the mother country could offer, and no notice was taken of him, even if British imports did vary in quality.

America's first great actress was Charlotte Cushman (1816–76). Whitman thought her the best living player and, indeed, when she returned from five years on the English stage she proved a major actress. That she acted Romeo regularly

Left: Edwin Forrest became a fine actor after a crude start. He was a very powerful performer.

was partly due to her appropriate looks, partly because she clearly acted the part very well.

Charlotte Cushman was the first American Lady Gay Spanker in Dion Boucicault's *London Assurance* (1841). Revived in 1972 by the Royal Shakespeare company, with Donald Sinden unforgettable as the ruins of a Regency rake, Sir William Harcourt Courtly, its author was a considerable man of the theatre on both sides of the Atlantic. His career fabulously sums up the mid-Victorian theatre at its liveliest. Born in Dublin in 1822, he became an Anglo-American with an extraordinary flair for theatrical effect. Many of his

plays were adapted from the French. His most famous ones were *The Corsican Brothers*, a romantic melodrama called *The Coleen Bawn*, *The Streets of London* and *The Octoroon*. In the United States *The Streets of London* became *The Streets of New York* – having been originally borrowed from the French *Les Pauvres de Paris*.

Boucicault also acted, introduced matinées, gave Charles Kean a runaway hit with the melodrama *The Corsican Brothers*, and wrote a very popular Irish melodrama called *Arrah-na-Pogue*. The box-set and fireproof scenery were invented by him, and, though a plagiarist, he suggested that the U.S. Congress should allow authors to be protected by copyright. His stage effects included the Derby, the Oxford and Cambridge Boat Race and he brought Irving to London. He formed the first touring company in the modern sense – sending out a West End cast on tour, with his *Colleen Bawn*, which opened in Sunderland on 4 February 1861. His real name was Dionysius Lardner Boursiquot and his *The Shaughraun*, in which he played the irresponsible Con, was the most popular play of the nineteenth century. He also achieved bigamy and the admiration of Queen Victoria.

His *The Octoroon*, which was first staged in 1859, was the first play to treat the subject of the American negro and slavery seriously. Of course, it was also a splendid show, complete with a burning Mississippi riverboat. A modern revival inevitably produced laughter and smiles. Little known today, three nations should be proud of him.

By this time theatres were springing up in America wherever there were towns. The gold rush areas – many far from California – were typical in that most towns had splendid theatres and 'opry houses'. Railroads would soon carry companies across the nation, a more comfortable ride than in a stagecoach. Lillie Langtry was one of those who had her own train. So did Colonel Mapleson's opera company from London in the 1880s. A century ago even modest little towns had theatres and expected, and often got, what would be termed today superstars.

During most of the nineteenth century a uniquely American form of entertainment, later immortalized by Jerome Kern in *Showboat*, was flourishing on the Mississippi, the Ohio and several other

great rivers. Steamboats had started plying the Mississippi as early as 1811, and the first actors known to have used boats did so in 1817, but actually performed on shore. They sailed along the Cumberland to the Mississippi in the *Noah's Ark*, which belonged to the enterprising Noah Ludlow. By the 1830s there were real showboats in action, and, except during the civil war, when many were enlisted into the Confederate Navy, they prospered mightily. Some of the captains had a genius for making the most of their ships, notably Henry Butler, who displayed waxworks by day and presented rousing dramas each evening. Nautical dramas were especially popular, the most famous – on both sides of the Atlantic – being *Black Eyed Susan*.

The first real showboat was the brainchild of a London and New York actor named William Chapman, who called his craft the *Floating Palace*. As late as the 1940s these exotic craft were still in action, presenting the new-fangled musical comedies more often than the grand old melodramas so associated with the floating theatres. Some sank or blew up from time to time – it was in the nature of steamboats to do so, but they were an integral and glamorous part of the Western scene.

Exciting and romantic as the showboats seem, they were peripheral theatre. The nation's theatre capital was naturally New York. Washington, so long did it take to be built from nothing, even now cannot compete with New York as a centre of the

Right: T.P. Cooke in Black Eyed Susan, *which ran for 400 performances. Before acting in melodramas he had been a Jack Tar.*

Left: Edwin Booth was the greatest of an acting family and remains America's supreme actor. He was much admired in Britain.

arts. Boston, however, was a major centre, a new theatre opening in 1854 with room for 3,500 patrons. It was here that in the 1860s Edwin Booth played Macbeth opposite a German Lady Macbeth who spoke her native language on stage, a happening more common in opera than in the straight theatre.

Booth is widely regarded as America's greatest Shakespearean actor, an outstanding tragedian, the most brilliant member of a very talented family. His father, Junius Brutus Booth (1796–1852) was born in London. His Richard III was enough like Edmund Kean's to produce rival Keanites and Boothites, but he once played Iago to Kean's Othello. He went to America in 1821, managing Baltimore's Adelphi Theatre and introducing Charles Kean to the American public. He died on a Mississippi steamboat. A grand actor rather than a polished one, he was somewhat unbalanced, perhaps from drink, but he, more than anyone, established the tradition of tragic acting in America.

Booth had ten children, one of whom, John Wilkes, assassinated Abraham Lincoln. His eldest son, Junius Brutus, was also an actor, but is best remembered as a manager and producer.

Edwin Thomas Booth (1833–93) was a glorious actor in the tradition of Edmund Kean. He had presence, a beautiful voice, intelligence and sustained power. Lacking height, he was able to seem tall. He had to bear not only the continuing nightmare of his brother's infamous deed, but also a

Above: One of Booth's most famous parts was Iago. He and Irving alternated Iago and Othello at the Lyceum.

retired after his brother's crime, but returned nearly a year later because the public demanded it.

Bankruptcy in 1873 did not deter him: he toured the U.S.A. with great success. He travelled to London and Germany in the early 1880s, a highlight of which tour was appearances at the Lyceum alternating Othello and Iago with Irving. The critic Dutton Cook summed them up by writing: 'We have here two simply masterly Iagos, two insufficient Othellos.'

Booth died in 1893, the year William Winter wrote a most perceptive tribute to his art. Having stressed his physical advantages and the way that his nobility of presence was later 'softened and hallowed by experience and grief', he went on:

Alike in youth and age, in bloom and in decline, he was exceptional and rare ... He needed not to seek after novelty: he was himself a novelty. The old plays were adequate for his purpose, because, in his inspired expression of their thought and feeling, character and action, he made them ever new ... The salient attributes of Booth's art were imagination, insight, grace, intense emotion, and melancholy refinement. In Hamlet, Richelieu, Othello, Iago, King Lear ... they were conspicuously manifest. But the controlling attribute – that which imparted individual character, colour and fascination by his acting – was the thoughtful introspective habit of stately mind, abstracted from passion and suffused with mournful dreaminess of temperament. The moment the charm began to work, his victory was complete. It was that which made him the true image of Shakespeare's thought ...

This exceptional actor was a founder member of the New York Players Club. He donated a house for it and it was founded in 1888 along the lines of London's Garrick Club. It is a treasure trove of theatrical mementoes and pictures.

While Boucicault was going from strength to strength on both sides of the Atlantic, other American playwrights were vying with their British colleagues to entertain the public. *Uncle Tom's Cabin*, based faithfully on the hugely influential book about slavery, was a colossal success, while Britain gave America that lachrymose melodrama *East Lynne* by Mrs Henry Wood, though the play's most famous line does not appear in her novel – 'Dead! and ... never called me mother'.

streak of insanity in his father, his brother and his second wife.

He first appeared in Boston in 1849 when he was 16, playing the tiny part of Tyrell in *Richard III*. He had the long training so invaluable and so rare today. He played Richard III at 18, going on for his father with no great success, then toured Australia with Laura Keene, an English actress and manager, in 1854, an unsuccessful venture. He gave a superb Richard III in New York in 1857, was seen as Shylock and Sir Giles Overreach at the Haymarket in London in 1861, then caused a sensation by playing Hamlet for 100 consecutive performances in 1864 in New York, a record not broken until John Barrymore achieved 101 in 1922. He

In fact, much worse plays than that were being turned out, the equivalent of dire dime novels about Western heroes. Better were the superior costume dramas, notably *The Count of Monte Cristo* in which James O'Neill toured for so long and which his son would recall in *Long Day's Journey into Night*.

Things got better with Bronson Howard (1842–1908), the first full-time American dramatist, who not only used American characters and themes, but also founded the American Dramatists Club. He also improved the laws of copyright. His first hit, *Saratoga*, opened in 1870 and concerned a man about town who loved 'not wisely but four well'. He followed this with satirical plays and dramas, the

Above: A scene from Under the Gaslight *(New York, 1867). Brave Laura has escaped from captivity. Will she save her friend?*

Left: The beautiful Maxine Elliott acted in Europe and Australia as well as her native America. She is seen here in Myself, Bettina *(New York, 1908).*

most successful being *The Young Mrs. Winthrop*.

Also popular was the prolific William Clyde Fitch (1865–1909) who wrote 50 plays, many as star vehicles, including *Her Own Way* in 1903 for Maxine Elliott, the 'Venus with Arms'.

Fitch wrote a number of sub-Ibsen dramas, including *The City*, but it was his comedies and romances that made his name at home and abroad, including *Beau Brummell* and *Captain Jinks of the Horse Marines*. He once had four plays running on Broadway and also had the honour of being closed by New York's police, when Olga Nethsole in his *Sappho* was carried upstairs by the hero to a fate worse than death.

A famous figure on both sides of the Atlantic was the outstanding manager, Augustin Daly. He wrote Westerns for the stage, translated Sardou and Dumas and others into English, presented Shakespeare and opened a number of theatres. Daly's in London opened in 1893 with *The Taming of the Shrew* starring the American John Drew and

Ada Rehan, her Katherine being her most acclaimed role. Daly's in London was famous for its musical comedies.

John Drew was one of a family that could trace its acting back to Elizabethan England. He and his actress wife had three children, the youngest of whom married Maurice Barrymore, the English actor and father of America's most famous Hamlet, John Barrymore, the magnificent Ethel Barrymore and the fine character actor, Lionel Barrymore. After a success in *The Copperhead* in 1918, he concentrated on films. To a great extent the old Anglo-American theatre was a family affair.

The Barrymores belong to our century, a century that at last saw the American stage graced by many very fine and some great plays. The playwrights of nineteenth-century America had mainly been British or Anglo-American. From the 1900s, for all the close links between the American and British theatres, Broadway and the West End, the American stage found its own unique identity.

Below: Augustin Daly bestrode the Atlantic like a Colossus. He opened several New York theatres and the famous Daly's in London, presenting plays and musicals including The Maid of the Mountains *and* The Merry Widow.

The Rise of
MODERN DRAMA

Scandinavia

Received theatre wisdom has it that Henrik Ibsen was the father of modern drama. It is by no means controversial to regard him as second only to Shakespeare. His influence has been colossal – his masterful use of the climax, his sparing but inspired use of symbolism at key moments, his superb characterization. Professor Richard Vowles has claimed him as the father of the modern problem play, noting how he turned the well-made play into a compact, classical vehicle.

Yet the odd fact about the Norwegian genius is that only a small proportion of his plays are ever performed outside Scandinavia, and many are not even seen there. It is possible for a regular playgoer outside Scandinavia never to see the two best-known of his early plays, *Peer Gynt* and *Brand*.

Ibsen was born into a wealthy family in the small coastal town of Skien in 1828. His father later went bankrupt and Ibsen, aged 15, was apprenticed to a druggist.

The outline facts of his career are that he become literary editor of the National Theatre at Bergen in 1851, then the Director of the Norske Theatre at Christiana (1857–62), after which a state pension gave him financial security. It was an enlightened and unusual gesture.

Ibsen moved from historical and verse dramas to apparently naturalistic social plays, which he constructed with consummate skill. His last plays were even more densely symbolic than his very early ones, indeed symbolism is never completely absent from his work, even from his most realistic plays. That humour is limited in his works makes his achievement even more remarkable. The critic, Michael Billington, has called him a passionate believer in spiritual regeneration and a master builder whose plays are perfectly structured pieces of architecture. His plays are high art, however, not to be confused with the merely 'well-made' play. Yet the best of that genre owe him a debt.

After *Cataline* (1850), inspired by Scribe and Schiller, he wrote the historical dramas, *The Vikings at Helgeland* and *The Pretenders*, but the first play which is still fairly regularly given is *Peer Gynt* (1867), a wonderful poetic fantasy-drama with a reckless, richly human hero. A year earlier *Brand*, the play that won him his pension, was published, although it was not staged until 1885. It is a bleak, vast, symbolic drama about a fanatical pastor who sacrifices his family for his ministry.

Left: The face of the revolutionary who changed theatrical history and who gave actors and actresses so many fine parts, Henrik Ibsen.

From the 1870s Ibsen wrote a string of masterpieces, including *A Doll's House*, his most performed play outside Norway, in which a woman finds fulfilment by abandoning her husband and children. *Ghosts* dared to tackle the subject of venereal disease and was first staged in 1882 in Chicago. It inspired the *Daily Telegraph*'s critic, Clement Scott, to call it 'an open drain, a loathsome sore', whereas it is actually a harrowing tragedy. Municipal corruption is attacked in *An Enemy of the People*, but the attack is seen through Doctor Stockmann who dares to tell the truth about a polluted spa. Ibsen launched his messages through people, not propaganda.

In 1884 came *The Wild Duck*, for many Ibsen's masterpiece. The playwright uses mysterious symbolism to sympathize with characters who create a virtual nature reserve in an attic, while he bitterly attacks the intellectual, Gregers Werle, whose determination to reveal the truth leads to tragedy. *Rosmersholm* has the 'new woman', Rebecca West, as its heroine and it ends in a double suicide.

There followed *Hedda Gabler*, whose bored destructiveness leads to her own self-destruction, a famous part in a play where all the characters are finely drawn. It was now 1890 and Ibsen was at the height of his powers. *The Master Builder* has a hero whose virility is waning until Hilde Wangel makes a memorable entrance. The sexual symbolism of Master Builder Solness and the tower he is building comes through strongly. *John*

Above: Cheryl Campbell and Stephen Rea in Strindberg's Miss Julie.

Opposite: Janet Suzman as Hedda Gabler. *She is also a noted Shakespearean, her Cleopatra being especially fine.*

Gabriel Borkman portrays a man whose lust for power leads him to sacrifice love. As in *Little Eyolf*, and Ibsen's last play, *When We Dead Awaken*, symbolism becomes an even more dominant force.

In his own lifetime Ibsen's realistic plays were the most influential. Now Ibsen's poetical qualities are appreciated, and the power of his symbolism, while his skill in building up to climaxes holds most audiences in his thrall. He has influenced even those dramatists who have rejected him.

Michael Meyer, Ibsen's biographer, has written that 'Isaiah, dressed in a tall hat and a morning coat would surely have looked and talked like Ibsen'. In a 150th birthday tribute Michael Billington, having quoted this daunting picture, reminded his readers that Ibsen the dramatist is bracing, perplexing and perennially inescapable.

Norway's other playwright of note in the nineteenth century was Bjornstjerne Bjornson (1832–1910), who was more popular in his own time then Ibsen. His finest play is possibly *Mary Stuart in Scotland*, and he wrote a number of social dramas. *Beyond Human Power* examines the danger of too much idealism. He was the first Scandinavian to win a Nobel Prize. Little performed today, he is revered as a patriot and fighter against injustice.

August Strindberg (1849–1912), Sweden's greatest playwright, is understandably regarded as a notable mysogynist. However, he liked domesticity enough to sample it with three wives, even if his personality made for tempestuous relationships.

These are reflected in a number of lethal dramas. He had started by writing rural farcical comedies, the best-known being *Lucky Peter's Travels*. In 1887 a sudden volcanic change came with *The Father* in which an army officer is locked in a ferocious struggle with his more strong-willed wife. It ends with him in a strait-jacket, dying of a stroke. This is Strindberg's first public and titanic battle of the sexes, a battle the man must always lose. His searing plays are strong meat for actors and audiences. Strindberg claimed that his next play, *Miss Julie*, was the first naturalistic Scandinavian drama, with an aristocratic woman and a footman as the protagonists. He wrote 15 historical plays, the vast *To Damascus*, the expressionist *Dream Play* and many others. However, the most widely known of his later plays are *The Dance of Death* and *The*

Ghost Sonata. The former portrays a marriage riven by hate as it nears its silver wedding. Edgar, the army officer husband, is as famous a role as it is taxing, and the wife is another unforgettable creation. (There was an awe-inspiring production of the play by the National Theatre at the Old Vic in 1967, with Olivier, Geraldine McEwen and Robert Stephens. Edgar is one of the most demanding roles in modern drama.) The play is not for weaklings and must be acted by titans. *The Ghost Sonata* is one of the dramatist's 'chamber plays' and is filled with grotesques; appearance is contrasted with sordid reality. Thornton Wilder called Strindberg the 'fountainhead of virtually all modernism in the drama'. Strindberg knew himself. When asked what the predominant trait in his character was he answered that it was his strange mixture

Below: Anton Chekhov and his actress wife Olga Knipper-Chekhova, who created some of his great roles.

of the deepest pessimism and utter recklessness. His motto was *speravit infestis* – he hoped in adversity.

Russia

It was Peter the Great who first allowed Russian audiences to see Western plays. He imported a German company and established the St. Petersburg Imperial Theatre in his newly built capital in 1702. Russians could now see the work of leading French and other dramatists, while Johann Kunst, who led the German company, trained Russian actors to perform in the imported plays.

In 1782, Denis Fonvizin's *The Minor*, a thoughtful and entertaining play, virtually created Russia's realistic theatre. It is still popular and greatly influenced later Russian masters. The hero is an oafish lad

of 16, and many parts of the dialogue have entered Russian speech, most notably: 'I don't want to study, I want to marry.'

There followed Alexander Griboyedov (1795–1829), a popular and lively writer of comedies, and Nikolai Gogol, whose *The Inspector General* (1836) is still well known and revived in many countries. An hilarious attack on Russian bureaucracy, it is considered an attack on Tsarist rule in today's Soviet Union. Turgenev's *A Month in the Country*, first performed in 1872, two decades after it was written, is still popular far beyond the Soviet Union, while Alexander Ostrovsky (1823–86) remains Russia's most prolific playwright. He also helped in running Moscow's Maly (small) Theatre. His *The Storm* is well known outside the U.S.S.R. (also in operatic form by Janacek as *Katya Kabanova*) and his *The Forest* made a great

impression when staged by the Royal Shakespeare Company in 1981. He was one of the most important figures of the Russian theatre of his day.

There followed the greatest of all Russian playwrights, Anton Chekhov (1860–1904). His plays are loved by countless theatregoers in whose affections he is surely only second to Shakespeare. It needed some time for actors, then audiences, to understand him. That appreciation was promoted by two great men of the theatre who founded the Moscow Art Theatre in 1898: the actor, director and teacher Constantin Stanislavsky and the director and co-founder of the theatre, Vladimir Nemirovich-Danchenko.

It was Stanislavsky who directed Chekhov's supreme masterpieces, *The Seagull, Uncle Vanya, The Three Sisters*

Above: A scene from the first Uncle Vanya *with Stanislavsky (third right) as Astrov and Chekhov's wife (second right) as Elena.*

and *The Cherry Orchard* between 1899 and 1904. This quartet, if less wide ranging, matches that other quartet of imperishable glory, *Hamlet*, *Othello*, *Macbeth* and *King Lear*.

The plays of Chekhov, so subtle, moving and naturalistic, needed actors who rejected the broad methods of the day. Complete naturalism in acting – simulating the illusion of reality – was sought and found. Settings and costumes had to be authentic as well, and rehearsals went on for longer than most theatres, however dedicated, could possibly allow.

Stanislavsky's writings, *An Actor Prepares*, *Building a Character*, *My Life in Art* and *Stanislavsky Rehearses Othello*, are a most valuable quartet, and gave those who could not work with him a clear view of his beliefs. Few would have so long to rehearse as he and his company had, but all could benefit by his emphasis on hard work and keen observation of humanity.

Chekhov's characters, mostly upper middle class, experience every human emotion from abandoned gaiety to total despair, but for many years, helped by parodies, they were felt by some to be gloom-laden and humourless. Yet the four most famous plays, plus other earlier full-length ones, *Platanov*, *Ivanov* and *The Wood Demon*, are a dazzling treasure trove of humanity. It is not easy to analyse his unique talent. Plots appear loosely drawn, yet he worked on them with exceptional care. He once said to a novice: 'If a gun is hanging on the wall in the first act, it must be fired in the last.' Yet the most significant part of any Chekhov play is the effect that the characters exert on each other. He was a supreme master of situation, atmosphere and character, while no playwright has known better what to include, what to leave out. A Russian is likely to detect in him a prophet foreseeing a heroic future. One

Above: John Hurt and Natasha Richardson in Chekhov's The Seagull *at the Lyric Hammersmith in 1985.*

Opposite: Peter Ashmore's 1951 production of The Three Sisters, *a legendary event with Richardson as Vershinin and, left to right, Renee Asherson, Celia Johnson and Margaret Leighton as Irina, Olga and Masha.*

may suggest that only a stupendous genius could make audiences care deeply, sometimes desperately, about whether or not a cherry orchard should be sold, or about the three sisters, Olga, Masha and Irina, longing so deeply for a Moscow that they will never reach.

Maxim Gorky (1868–1936) was the most gifted of Chekhov's contemporaries. His *The Lower Depths* had its premiére at the Moscow Art Theatre in 1902 and he was acclaimed by Chekhov for being the first to express his contempt for the petit bourgeois and choosing the right moment to do so. The setting is a

Below: Oscar Wilde, playwright, poet, author and wit.

cellar in Moscow's underworld, a refuge for derelicts, and the theme that of accepting lies or facing the truth. Gorky wrote 14 plays between 1902 and 1915, including *Summerfolk* and *Enemies*. He left Russia in the 1920s, returning to write three more plays. Some believe that he was later murdered by the state.

Britain

The English stage, the British stage, or the Anglo-Irish stage (the first historically correct, the second and, especially the third, more accurate at this period) did not produce a contemporary playwright to equal Chekhov or Ibsen. Yet after a period of sterility from the death of

Sheridan, it recovered itself, thanks very largely to Irishmen.

His fellow Irishman, Oscar Wilde (1854–1900) achieved theatrical immortality with *The Importance of Being Earnest*, a masterpiece of wit and construction worthy of Congreve, which appeared in 1895. His other plays, *Lady Windermere's Fan*, *A Woman of No Importance* and *An Ideal Husband*, have been fairly regularly revived, but these epigram-studded society dramas are not to be compared with *The Importance*. He also wrote *Salomé*, which in its German translation provided Richard Strauss with the libretto of his first great success. Wilde's trial and imprisonment for homosexuality happened in the same year as *The*

Importance's first production. *Salomé* was banned in England, but staged in France in 1896 under the aegis of Sarah Bernhardt.

Arthur Wing Pinero (1855–1934) was a prolific playwright, whose serious plays, most notably *The Second Mrs Tanqueray*, starring Mrs Patrick Campbell, were once hugely successful. However, he lives on today for two farces, *The Magistrate* and *Dandy Dick*, but above all for *Trelawny of the 'Wells'* a warm and loving and entertaining re-creation of the theatre of the 1860s.

The prolific George Bernard Shaw (1856–1950) wrote 57 plays in all, many of them with their own preface (sometimes more lively than the plays). He had great

Right: Bernard Shaw 'attacking' Harley Granville-Barker, whose wife Lillah McCarthy is between them. Androcles and the Lion *is being rehearsed.*

Below: Saint Joan *at the New Theatre in 1947, the Old Vic's production directed by John Burrell. Celia Johnson is Joan, Alec Guinness (left) the Dauphin and John Clements Dunois.*

assets: an exhilarating mastery of the language, dazzling wit, a cornucopia of ideas, a determination to tease and to shock – though not to excess. In an age of censorship he rightly wanted to be heard. He was at one time an art critic and was a major music critic, at once readable (of course) and very well informed. Despite the hostility of some, many of his plays have never been out of the repertory, and he has his own festival at Niagara-on-the-Lake, Ontario. Accusations of his untheatricality have some validity. His truly theatrical moments – *coups du théâtre* – are undeniably rare. 'How long, O Lord, how long?' asks Joan at the end of *Saint Joan*, and we are moved, despite the high jinks we have just enjoyed in the Epilogue of the play.

Indebted to Ibsen, he repaid his debt with *The Quintessence of Ibsenism* and in the plays *Mrs Warren's Profession* and *Widowers' Houses* and, perhaps, *Candida* (1895). Other plays of the very fertile nineties include the short and entertaining *The Man of Destiny*, about the young Napoleon, the delicious *You Never Can Tell* and the entertaining *Caesar and Cleopatra*.

The Royal Court Theatre, destined in the 1950s to become the most important in Britain for a number of heady years, had such an important early history that Shaw's career must be interrupted to put a most fertile part of it in its historical context. The theatre replaced an older one in Sloane Square and opened in 1888.

Ten years later Pinero's *Trelawny of the 'Wells'* gave it the boost of a major hit. In 1904 the manager John Vedrenne and the director Harley Granville-Barker took the theatre over.

Granville-Barker had taken part in William Poel's production of *Richard II* for the Elizabethan Stage Society in 1899, four years after this influential actor-manager had founded it. He presented *Twelfth Night* in 1895 on a reconstruction of an Elizabethan stage, swiftly and simply, worlds away from the usual elaborate productions of the time. Granville-Barker would later put his mentor's precepts to brilliant use in a series of Shakespearean productions at the Savoy Theatre from 1912–14, staging them simply and with great poetic beauty, a sign of things to come very different from the staging extravagances in vogue.

At the Royal Court, however, it was Granville-Barker's productions of modern drama that were so crucially important. Barker had played Marchbanks in the original *Candida* in 1900, being chosen by Shaw himself. Now Barker presented *Captain Brassbound's Conversion* for the Stage Society, also *Mrs Warren's Profession* and *Man and Superman* between 1900 and 1905, his wife, Lillah McCarthy, starring with him

in the last of these. The Society could produce plays unlicensed by the all-powerful Lord Chamberlain, whose office vetted all new plays for public performance, so *Mrs Warren*, with its theme of prostitution, could escape his rule. Granville-Barker virtually retired in 1921, concentrating on his very influential *Prefaces to Shakespeare*.

Meanwhile Shaw's monumental output continued at awesome speed. He now developed his idea of the Life-Force in *Man and Superman* and there followed *John Bull's Other Island*, on Ireland, *Major Barbara* and *The Doctor's Dilemma*, a witty attack on the medical profession. The short *Androcles and the Lion* is dwarfed by a huge preface on Christianity. *Pygmalion*, with Mrs Patrick Campbell far too old but superb as Eliza Doolittle, opened in 1914. There followed *Heartbreak House*, a play of depth which is highly regarded, the overlong *Back to Methuselah* and, apart from his masterpiece *Saint Joan*, a succession of lesser works, only *The Apple Cart*, a political comedy, being truly Shavian.

Many of the follies he exposed are now gone, while in some plays, notably *Getting Married*, the characters are simply talking horses. Yet he could create brilliant characters, one of his finest being General Burgoyne in *The Devil's Disciple*, who, however, virtually wrecks the play, having more vitality than the rest of the characters put together. It was first seen in New York in 1897, with the dashing Richard Mansfield in the lead. Yet Shaw's genius for showing that ideas can entertain never left him, even when characterization is lacking. His last play, *Far-Fetched Fables*, was in 1950, the year of his death. As for his command of language, he ranks as one of the great masters of English prose.

Shaw's career in the theatre began in Irving's day, when the actor-manager was still in the ascendant: giants like Irving, Herbert Beerbohm Tree (the first Professor Higgins), Martin-Harvey, Forbes-Robertson and many more, including those who spent their lives on tour. The actor-manager was still his own director, though it must be stressed again that until the 1960s in Britain the director was confusingly known as the producer. (The American practice is now used, the producer being the person who puts the show on.)

The old-time actor-manager, good or bad, was summed up by the playwright Ronald Jeans as 'one to whom the part is greater than the whole'. The last of the great ones was Sir Donald Wolfit, who toured Shakespeare for many valiant years, and who inspired Ronald Harwood's 1980 play *The Dresser*.

In 1908 Britain's first repertory theatre was opened by Annie Horniman, a rich Victorian who had previously re-opened the Abbey Theatre in Dublin as the Repertory Theatre of Ireland in 1903. In Manchester she presented 200 plays, half of which were new ones, an astounding achievement, before being forced to close in 1921. One was Harold Brighouse's *Hobson's Choice*. Ben Iden Payne was her gifted director. He was a disciple of William Poel and later became an influential Shakespearean director and teacher in America.

It was Miss Horniman who established the pattern of British repertory, which down the years performed a different play for a week, a fortnight, three, four, sometimes five weeks throughout the year. Outside Britain the word repertory describes the repertoire of plays that a company gives over a season – as at the National Theatre, the Royal Shakespeare etc.

Below: Peter O'Toole as Higgins and Jackie Smith-Wood as Eliza with Jack Watling and Lally Bowers in Pygmalion *in 1984. In 1986 O'Toole was a superb King Magnus in* The Apple Cart, *a role he first played at the Bristol Old Vic.*

Above: A beautiful picture of Sarah Bernhardt, who was admired far beyond France.

pallor spread over the features; the eyes became bloodshot; the hair hung dishevelled over the brow; the jaw shook nervously; the brand of Cain was seen on the face of this terror-stricken creature, and she who but a few minutes before was brightened into beauty with love became haggard and hideous with crime.

Bernhardt's Cleopatra in the play of that name was too vivid for some if a famous story is to be believed: The Divine Sarah was giving her all in London in 1892, finishing off by destroying her palace and, as the curtain started to fall, she collapsed in the wreckage. The audience was regularly sent into a transport of frenzy by this exhibition, but not a staid middle-aged lady, who said to her husband: 'How different, how very different, from the home life of our own dear Queen!'

Bernhardt was one of the greatest-ever stars of the Comédie-Française, first appearing there in 1862. However, her stays there were stormy. She reached the pinnacle of her profession with her Phèdre and Dona Sol in *Hernani*. In 1899 she became manager of the Théâtre Sarah Bernhardt. She was a famous Hamlet, excelled in Rostand's *L'Aiglon* (The Eaglet) about Napoleon's son, and was a writer, a poet and a painter. She was also a patriot: she refused to visit Germany after France's defeat in 1870 despite fabulous offers. She was once asked what her terms were for appearing in Berlin. She telegraphed back: 'Alsace-Lorraine'! She died in 1923. Primitive films do her no justice because her acting was so passionate and fluid – unlike her great Italian contemporary Eleanora Duse, whose acting was slow, still and subtle. London saw both in 1895, Shaw hailing Duse, Clement Scott Bernhardt. Happy the age that could enjoy both, often in the same roles.

France

In the French theatre Victorien Sardou (1831–1908) succeeded Scribe and wrote an exceptionally wide range of 'well-made' plays. Bernard Shaw rudely described them as 'Sardoodledum'. *La Tosca*, which inspired Puccini's opera, is the best known of his plays outside France. It was one of Sarah Bernhardt's famous parts, as was the title role in his *Fédora*, both being constantly revived.

The 'Divine Sarah' was born in 1844. In *Theodora* in London in 1887, she moved the *Daily Telegraph* critic to write:
(it) was wonderful that so slight and frail a woman could command such a thrill of excitement. The murder settled and inevitable, the whole face and physique seemed to undergo a change. A deadly

Italy

Duse was particularly successful in the plays of her fellow countryman Gabriele D'Annunzio, whose most dramatic play is *La figlia di Jorio* (Jorio's Daughter). In *La Gioconda* (Mona Lisa) Duse starred opposite the great Italian actor Tommaso Salvini. D'Annunzio was a dashing fighter in the First World War. His seizure of the port of Fiume – which the Italian Government did not want – was more dramatic than any of his plays.

Other notable French actresses were Réjane, who was a superb light

M. HENRI LAVEDAN   Mme SARAH BERNHARDT   Dessin de C. LÉANDRE.

Left: Bernhardt in Varennes. Her Hamlet went down better in France than in Britain, where she was usually adored.

comedienne, and the Italian Ristori, whom Mrs Kendal, herself a noted actress, considered even more remarkable than Bernhardt because she triumphed without sex appeal. There was also a magnificent Polish actress, Helena Modjeska, a major tragedienne who emigrated to America in 1876.

Italy's most famous actor in the late nineteenth century was Tommaso Salvini, who died in his seventies in 1915. He was especially famous as Othello, an electric but restrained performance which was widely admired. We have the word of Henry James for the restraint, the novelist calling him 'magnificently quiet' and noting the total lack of rant or crudity. The Press tried to create trouble between him and Irving, but failed. A fine-looking, strongly built man with a beautiful voice, he was much approved of by Stanislavsky who noted that he arrived at the theatre three hours early to prepare himself for his roles. His Hamlet was successful in England, his Macbeth in Scotland.

Russia and the ballet

The great Russian Ballets Russes had an extraordinary effect on the performing arts in the early years of the century. Since the Romantic era ballet had been debased, even in Russia, men's roles often being danced by women. The ballerina was totally in command and even the genius of Tchaikovsky could not halt the decline.

Ballet was saved by an organizer of genius, Serge Diaghilev, who was neither dancer nor choreographer, but a man of great taste and drive. He gathered a superb team around him that remains unequalled, including perhaps the greatest of all choreographers, Mikhail Fokine, and the artists Bakst and Benois. His composers included Stravinsky, and his incomparable dancers were headed by Nijinsky, Karsavina, Bohm and Pavlova. This was the Ballets Russes.

Fokine and Diaghilev wanted a totally theatrical blend of music, dancing, painting and acting, and they achieved it. Diaghilev also created an opera company. It was very fine although not in the same class, and performed Russian masterpieces unknown in Western Europe. It included the incomparable actor-singer Chaliapin, whose Boris Godunov is one of the most famous and legendary performances in theatre history.

The Ballets Russes burst on Paris and Western Europe in 1909: the Polovstian Dances from *Prince Igor* were so electrifying that the rail was torn away from the front of the orchestra by the audience. The designers Bakst and Benois also triumphed, and their influence extended far beyond the world of ballet. Diaghilev and his amazing ensemble astounded both the world of the theatre and of art. By the 1920s he was using Picasso, Braque and Matisse and others, who revelled in their opportunities with backcloths and scenic effects in general.

America

Stars from Europe continued to flock to America, some like Lillie Langtry being more famous for their beauty than their talent, and in her case, her Royal connections.

Salvini was seen to advantage, even playing the Ghost in *Hamlet* and also Othello to the Hamlet and Iago of Edwin Booth.

Sarah Bernhardt made a number of farewell tours and, as noted, Richard Mansfield, the swashbuckling American actor, gave America its first taste of George Bernard Shaw.

Naturally, the successors of the great Sir Henry Irving crossed the Atlantic, including the Kendals – who were a devoted couple on and off stage who helped raise the profession out of the rogues and vagabonds class. (There are those, thinking of the West End between the wars, who wish they had not, but at the time a touch of respectability did no harm.)

Sir Johnston Forbes-Robertson was another visitor to the U.S.A. He is generally regarded as the finest Hamlet of his day, and his most impressive modern part was the Stranger in *The Passing of the Third Row Back* (1908). His daughter Jean was to become a noted Shakespearean and the finest of all Peter Pans. She made her first appearance in New York in *As You Like It* opposite the American actress Mary Anderson. The latter played Rosalind at Stratford-upon-Avon, and she made history by doubling Hermione and Perdita in *The Winter's Tale* at the Lyceum in London. It must be said that her double act seems to have been a sensational rather than an artistic success. With Robert Hichens she wrote *The Garden of Allah*, based on his novel set in North Africa.

Left: The Italian Salvini as Othello, his most famous role. A powerful man with a superb voice, he was greatly admired in Europe and America.

Right: Alexandre Benois created this stunning design for Petrushka. He and Leon Bakst, twin giants of the Ballets Russes, influenced design far beyond the world of ballet.

152

*Right: Sir Johnston
Forbes-Robertson, the
leading Hamlet of his day.
His touring contemporary
was Sir Frank Benson, who
took Shakespeare all over
Britain.*

Music hall

The heyday of the British music hall was
from around 1850 to the First World
War. Drink was an essential part of the
entertainment. Changes in the law
lessened the link with drinking, but there
were always bars in the later halls. The
acts were so wide ranging that the word
Variety – much used – meant just that.
The fare was more varied in earlier times
than those in their fifties can now recall,
for there were often dramatic interludes –
one-act plays – by 'legitimate' actors and
actresses, also animal acts and, of course,
comedians, acrobats, dancers, magicians
and every kind of 'novelty' act. Until

music halls virtually vanished once
television started booming in the middle
fifties, music hall artists could either stick
to the halls or, at the appropriate time of
year, work in pantomime. The most
famous London pantomime for many
years was Drury Lane's. The main
transformation scene there was always a
marvel, improvements in stage lighting
making such visible scene changes even
more effective than before. The contents
of a pantomime remain a blend of fairy
tale – with *Cinderella* the most popular
story down the years – and a variety bill.

As for the 'halls', two of those who
helped 'make' them were The Great

Vance and George – 'Champagne Charlie' Leybourne (from the name of his most famous song). Early stars of the halls had played working class characters. Now some of the new generation of working class entertainers made their fortunes playing men-about-town – swells. The friendly rivalry between Leybourne and Vance led to a series of comic songs that worked their way through the wine list.

The most beloved, perhaps, of all music hall stars was Dan Leno who had began his career at the age of four as 'Little George the Infant Wonder contortionist and posturer'. All of five feet tall, he played the Dame in 15 successive Drury Lane pantomimes. He specialized in monologues delivered at a cracking pace. The small genius worked himself to death and died insane. There has never been such a star of music hall and pantomime. Marie Lloyd, herself a superstar before the term was coined, said that he had the saddest eyes in the whole world.

Other great stars included Vesta Tilley, the superb male impersonator, whose songs included 'Burlington Bertie' and 'Following in Father's Footsteps'; Little Tich, four and a half feet of him, but with huge boots, an inspired character comedian; Harry Champion, whose songs were most notably about food, including the famous 'Boiled Beef and Carrots', and a host of other stars. George Robey the 'Prime Minister of Mirth', lived to appear on television, and there was Albert – 'My Old Dutch' – Chevalier and Gus – 'If it Wasn't for the Houses in Between' – Elen.

There was also Marie Lloyd, born in 1870 and the queen of the halls. Her racy material and racier private life kept her out of the first Royal Command Performance in 1912 so she promptly staged her own 'by order of the British Public'. When she got into trouble with

Overleaf: Tom Browne (1872–1910) created this superb poster.

Below: The 'look' of a London music hall gallery at the turn of the century.

PANTOMIME

A

J. MILES & CO LTD LITHOS
68,70, WARDOUR ST LONDON.W.

WOOD AND ARTHUR COLLINS.

'She Sits among the Cabbages and Peas' she changed it to 'She Sits among the Cabbages and Leeks'. 'My Old Man' was one of her many hit songs.

Scotland's chief gifts to the halls were Harry Lauder, knighted later for his work in the First World War, whose 'I Love a Lassie' and other songs remain favourites, and Will Fyffe, whose character sketches have rarely been equalled. There was also that 'essence of eccentricity', Nellie Wallace.

Several later names, among many, must be reverently noted: Max Miller, the Cheeky Chappie who like Marie Lloyd was a comic genius and was often banned; Flanagan and Allen and the rest of the Crazy Gang, Bud Flanagan being a superb comedian; Sid Field, who was another; Will Hay, best known for his films; and, in no order of merit, Max Wall, George Formby and his ukelele; Tommy Trinder with his machine gun delivery; Tommy Cooper, a conjuror and joker who was the favourite of his fellow professionals; Frankie Howerd; and Ken Dodd, an entire variety performance in one body, who once told jokes for three hours, six

Left: Marie Lloyd (1870–1922) made her name with the song 'The Boy I Love is Up in the Gallery'. She became the queen of the halls and was also in pantomime. Her lyrics were sometimes censored, but she was always idolized by her audiences.

minutes and thirty seconds. On which awesome note we must cross the Atlantic.

Vaudeville

The word vaudeville derives from Vau-de-Vire in Normandy, where it referred to a kind of song popular in the fifteenth century aimed at the English invaders. The word later referred to performances in dumb show and with choruses, understandably often satirizing what went on in the grand theatre, of which the Comédie-Française had a monopoly. These later helped to develop the operettas that became so popular.

Meanwhile, to cater for respectable audiences, a performer-manager named Tony Pastor decided to clean up the American equivalent of variety. Pastor had started his career as a child performer with Phineas T. Barnum. Barnum, born in 1810, built his American Museum on Broadway in 1841, presenting spectacles and plays, every kind of oddity, and even culture with Jenny Lind the opera singer. General Tom Thumb (Charles Stratton) was among his stars. From 1871 he presented 'The Greatest Show on Earth',

his huge circus, which played every spring in New York, then toured.

Back in the mid-1860s Pastor, then in his mid-twenties, started his long campaign to reclaim vaudeville from drunks and prostitutes. He used several theatres, finally finding a home on Fourteenth Street, opening on 24 October 1881. There was to be no smoking or drinking and no excessive vulgarity. Pastor provided many of his own ballads.

This was a start – with eight typical acts, including singing, dancing, male impersonations, comedy and acrobatics. The silent screen had some adverse effect on vaudeville, the talkies far more so and radio and, especially, television, finished it off. Or did it? The cinema used the talents of vaudeville just as radio and television did and does. Tony Pastor had started something that could not be stopped. Yet because variety lasted so much longer in Britain than it did as vaudeville in America, it is perhaps best to leave the latter until the next chapter where it will form part of the story of Broadway, a more integral part than it did in the West End and beyond in the short while that it was in its prime.

Below: The poster says it all! The name Barnum is now known again to millions through the musical Barnum, *complete with Michael Crawford's staggering performance.*

WEST END, BROADWAY
and Beyond

Britain

Unlike during the Second World War, in which the performing arts thrived in Britain, First World War audiences demanded and got the lightest of entertainment. The ultimate hit was *Chu-Chin-Chow*, an oriental musical extravaganza that had music by Frederick Norton and a book by Oscar Asche based on Ali Baba and the Forty Thieves. It opened in August 1916 and was hugely popular with civilians and soldiers on leave alike.

Somerset Maugham, best known today as a short-story writer and novelist, had four plays running in the West End in 1908. After war service he reached his peak in the 1920s with *Home and Beauty*, *The Circle* and *The Constant Wife*, also, more seriously, *The Letter* in 1927 and the anti-war play *For Services Rendered*. After the comparative failure of *Sheppey* in 1933 he gave up writing for the theatre. His plays were serious compared with most other productions during and after the First World War.

Between the wars

Among much triviality, one person of outstanding importance, Lilian Baylis, was doing great things for the theatre. Born in 1874, this semi-educated, brave, God-intoxicated, earthy, glorious woman took over the running of the Old Vic in 1912 from her aunt, Emma Cons. The theatre, founded in 1818 as the Coburg, was turned into a temperance hall by Miss Cons in 1880. It was now the Victoria Theatre.

Lilian Baylis began to give opera and Shakespeare at popular prices. Her directors in the early days included Matheson Lang, Ben Greet, then Robert Atkins from 1921–25, a key period that established the reputation of the Old Vic, as it was always called. He directed the

as Shakespeare. Actors and singers were first British *Peer Gynt* as well as Shakespeare. Actors and singers were paid very little – Baylis prayed for good actors – and cheap – but serious actors and actresses were willing to work at the theatre, whose reputation steadily rose. Andrew Leigh took over direction, then, in a famous period, Harcourt Williams from 1929–33. It was at this time that the young John Gielgud established his fame as a classical actor, notably in such parts as Romeo, Richard II, Macbeth, Hotspur and Hamlet.

Without subsidy Baylis was a magnificent scrounger. Music was her subject, not theatre, but she knew enough and could spot talent. She would cook sausages in the wings and she produced the entire First Folio of Shakespeare's plays, the first to do so, between October 1914 and November 1923. When the Old Vic Company ended its glorious reign in 1963 the new National Theatre Company naturally moved in, while waiting for its own theatre building. She would undoubtedly be thrilled at the success of her beloved opera company, now the English National Opera.

In the West End Shakespeare had been considered unprofitable and Shakespearean acting ham. *Macbeth*, from Birmingham Repertory, slipped into the Royal Court in modern dress. Meanwhile, in 1931 Lilian Baylis reopened Sadler's Wells Theatre, a new building replacing a famous old theatre. Though her actors used it for a time, it was soon given to the young Sadler's Wells Opera, joined by the Sadler's Wells Ballet. This was another Baylis creation, led by Ninette de Valois, who had run the opera-ballet for her at the Old Vic, then actual ballets. Some of the promising stars were Robert Helpmann and Margot Fonteyn.

Right: Somerset Maugham's The Constant Wife, *revived in 1974, with Ingrid Bergman are Barbara Ferris and Michael Allinson.*

Right: Lilian Baylis (in glasses and gown) and company at Sadler's Wells. Among the galaxy are Charles Laughton, Flora Robson, Elsa Lancaster, James Mason and a towering Tyrone Guthrie.

At the Old Vic Tyrone Guthrie (1900–1971), the first Briton to become a world famous star director, was the theatre's youngest director in 1933 and returned in 1936–38.

Barry Jackson, a wealthy Midlander, had opened the Birmingham Rep in 1913, two years after the Liverpool Rep was founded. Liverpool was good, Birmingham was – and remained for many years – the best. Jackson would later start a Shaw festival at Malvern in 1929 and take over the Stratford-upon-Avon Shakespeare Memorial Theatre, as it was called, in 1945. He poured his own money into his Rep despite lack of support from Midlanders. He produced an extraordi-

nary range of pays by Molière, Ibsen, Galsworthy, George Kaiser and others, his directors including John Drinkwater and H. K. Ayliff. The most famous Shaw production was the first performance of *Back to Methuselah* in 1923, which was brought to London. No commercial management would have touched this vast work. Jackson adapted and translated foreign classics, staged opera and ballet in the early days of his reign, and employed, among others, Olivier, Richardson, Edith Evans, Peggy Ashcroft, Robert Newton, Cedric Hardwicke, Margaret Leighton, Paul Scofield, Albert Finney and Peter Brook – at the very start of the last's career. So notable was his reign from the beginning that he was knighted as early as 1925. His reign at the Shakespeare Memorial Theatre (1945–48) set it on its course to glory. He died in 1961. It is impossible to overstate his importance.

Laurence Olivier, born in 1907, joined the Birmingham Rep in 1926. His phenomenal career made him the inevitable choice for the first Director of the National Theatre when it finally opened at the Old Vic in 1963. He relinquished his post in 1973, the National Theatre opening on the South Bank under Peter Hall in 1976. Olivier was first spotted when he was only 14 by the great Ellen Terry, who saw him as Katharina in *The Taming of the Shrew*. 'Great' is a tricky word, even the most experienced theatregoers – and actors – arguing about who can achieve greatness, so whether Olivier is greater than Gielgud or the late Ralph Richardson is a matter of personal choice. Theatrically blessed is the country that had such a trio at the same time. Olivier's striking looks led to a fine screen career, but his loyalty to the theatre has never wavered. Inevitably he became the first theatrical life peer in 1970, having been knighted in 1948. Roles of his by which other actors are measured include Richard II, Henry V, Hotspur,

Left: Ralph Richardson as Face in Ben Jonson's The Alchemist *with the Old Vic at the New Theatre in 1947.*

163

Coriolanus, Othello, Astrov in *Uncle Vanya*, Titus Andronicus and also Macbeth, being one of the few actors to have – in most opinions – achieved greatness in the role. Minor delights have included his Tattle in *Love for Love* and Brazen in *The Recruiting Officer*. A sense of danger and electric excitement are two of his hallmarks. Like Richardson and Gielgud he will be appearing frequently in these pages.

Ralph Richardson (1902–84), like Olivier, was able to subsidize his ill-paid work at the Old Vic by West End and film appearances. The most famous Falstaff of modern times – with the Old Vic at the New Theatre in 1945 – this extraordinary and brilliant actor is renowned for portraying ordinary people. Two of his most notable performances in the 1930s were in Priestley plays, Charles Appleby in *Eden End* and the title-role in *Johnson over Jordan*. A dominating actor and a

*Left: Richardson and
Olivier as Falstaff and
Shallow in* Henry IV Part
II *with the Old Vic at the
New Theatre in 1945,
performances of ripe glory.*

brilliant comedian, one of his – and
Gielgud's – most memorable performances was in David Storey's *Home* in
1970.

John Gielgud, born in 1904 with Terry
blood in his veins, was the first of the
mighty trio to become famous and, more
importantly, a power in London. He
succeeded Noël Coward in *The Vortex*
(1925) and *The Constant Nymph* (1926),
and these and other commercial roles
enabled him to play for little money but
with great success at the Old Vic
(1929–31), as has been noted. This would
help him to bring Shakespeare back to the
West End in the 1930s after his long
banishment. In 1935 he presented *Romeo
and Juliet*, with himself and Olivier
alternating between Romeo and Mercutio. Their Juliet was Peggy Ashcroft,
born in 1907 and, as noted, a graduate of
the greatest of all Reps.

Two years later Gielgud would be
engaged in an even more important
venture, a classical season of quite
exceptional importance. First, however,

more must be said about the state of the West End theatre and its attitude to classical acting. By any standards the theatre was thriving, but underplaying, right enough in its place – middle and upper class dramas and comedies of the day – was not right for Shakespeare. The master of underplaying was Sir Gerald Du Maurier, who died in 1934. The difference between him and his many imitators, however, was that he was an incomparable performer, his restraint being much admired in Frederick Lonsdale's *The Last of Mrs Cheyney* and Sapper's *Bulldog Drummond*. True, John Barrymore's much-admired Hamlet had been acclaimed in London in 1925, but excellent as it was, it was not a bravura performance, while his personality and fame made the event fashionable despite the play being by Shakespeare.

Gielgud's poetic Hamlet in 1934 was greatly admired, a sign of the times, his *Romeo and Juliet* with its double casting causing a real stir. Yet the true test was about to come.

In the event, sanity was restored. The audience – a West End one – was ready for a season that was not only magnificent but is also regarded as the beginning of ensemble acting in Britain. (It should be noted that veterans claim that it was

Right: Gielgud's first Hamlet was in 1929, his last in 1944. For many theatre-goers he remains the Hamlet.

Left: Vernon Sylvaine had
two master farceurs as the
stars of his fine plays, little
Robertson Hare and big
bold Alfred Drayton – seen
here in Madame Louise,
with Hariette Johns.

started by Robert Atkins at the Old Vic in the 1920s.)

The Gielgud company, a true ensemble, was cast from experience, young talent and strength. The plays were *Richard II*, *The Merchant of Venice* and *The School for Scandal* but the season's summit seems to have been *The Three Sisters*, directed by Michel Saint-Denis and designed by Motley. It remains possibly the most famous production of a Chekhov play in Britain, and the one that finally established the playwright's growing popularity with British audiences. Gielgud was Vershinin; Gwen Ffrangcon-Davies, Carol Goodner and

Peggy Ashcroft, Olga, Masha and Irina; Angela Baddeley, Natasha; George Devine, Andrey; Glen Byam Shaw, Solyony; Michael Redgrave, Tusenbach; plus Harry Andrews, George Howe, Alec Guinness, Frederick Lloyd, Marie Wright and Barbara Dillon. Much postwar history of the British theatre would be in the hands of half of that extraordinary cast.

The West End rarely saw or sees quite such splendour, but it was in excellent health. Comedies and farces thrived, the finest being those at the Aldwych, by Ben Travers who had a hat-trick of hits in the mid-1920s with *A Cuckoo in the Nest*,

Overleaf: Terence
Rattigan's very fine
Separate Tables was
revived in 1976 with John
Mills, Jill Bennett and
Margaret Courtney
leading the company.

Opposite: *Noël Coward and Eva Gabor in* Present Laughter, *the master's last great comedy.*

Below: *Flora Robson was highly acclaimed in Lesley Storm's* Black Chiffon *in 1949. She also had notable successes in Shakespeare, Ibsen, Wilde and O'Neill.*

Rookery Nook and, above all *Thark*, which later found its way to the National Theatre. The genius of the house was Ralph Lynn, whose 'business' is still spoken of in awe. Excellent support came from Tom Walls and little Robertson Hare. He came into his own later in the farces of Vernon Sylvaine, teamed with the heavy, hairless Alfred Drayton. No-one has ever lost his trousers with such elan as Hare.

This was the period above all of Noël Coward, of his revues, musicals, songs, sophistication and of two of his three finest plays, in many of which he acted. The two are *Hay Fever* (1925) and *Private Lives* (1930), both seen later in New York. His third masterpiece is *Present Laughter* (1943), completing a trio worthy of Congreve. He wrote and composed songs and revues and musicals; he had some of his greatest successes opposite Gertrude

Lawrence, most notably in *Private Lives*. His early *The Vortex* (1924) had himself as the son of a drug addict played by Lilian Braithwaite.

Coward was a master of cabaret, revue, song and everything to do with the theatre, including being a fine director. He suffered a period of savage abuse in the aftermath of *Look Back in Anger* and its successors in the 1950s, and, indeed, his later plays were less fine, though always enjoyable. But he had the satisfaction of seeing *Hay Fever* at the National Theatre in 1964. His performances in films will show later generations just one side of his multi-talented flair that sometimes rose to the state of genius.

Terence Rattigan (1911–77) made his name with *French Without Tears* (1936), which ran for over 1,000 performances, and other successes included *The Winslow Boy*, an excellent drama based on an actual case, the amusing *While the Sun Shines*, and *The Browning Version*, a one-act tragedy about a failed schoolmaster, memorably played by Eric Portman. His finest play is *The Deep Blue Sea*, a 'searing study of the destructive zeal of love', so Tynan wrote. Praise has been heaped on players of the phoney major in *Separate Tables*, with the admittedly admirable David Niven winning an Oscar for his film performance but only a third-rate, miscast incompetent in a twice nightly rep could fail in the role. Rattigan suffered the same hostility as Coward late in his career and was less able to endure it. The tide has turned in his favour again to a lesser extent than Coward's change of fortunes, but the latter was the finer playwright. Rattigan just lived to see an improvement in his critical rating.

The British musicals of the inter-war years have not worn well: Coward's *Bitter Sweet* and the popular shows of Ivor Novello gave enormous pleasure, but show no sign of resurfacing.

Another feature of the inter-wars years was the growth of the repertory movement. Its origins have been traced earlier, but it deserves a few more comments. Few Reps could aspire to even the foothills of the leading companies, but much good work was done even by weekly Reps, along with bad. The killing routine of twice-nightly Rep was the most rugged discipline, professionalism coming fast, or the sack. Some veterans of such twice-nightly Rep became stars of *Coronation Street*, long service and good conduct medals indeed.

It is too common to hear old-time Rep sneered at, but many famous actors and actresses graduated from it, including Kenneth More, who learnt his craft in the most rugged circumstances. There were no subsidies then without which no Reps today could survive. The theatrical fact is that good Rep can make good actors better and bad Rep can give all but the most hopeless a decent smattering of technique. Besides, if the personality is right even the most unlikely have a chance to succeed.

Ireland

John Millington Synge (1871–1909) helped found the Irish Theatre movement, his masterpiece being *The Playboy of the Western World*. Like so many Irish plays of quality this was produced at the Abbey Theatre, Dublin, and it is about timid Christy Mahon, who is worshipped for allegedly killing his tyrannical father. It caused some of the worst riots in theatrical history. It was held to insult Irish womanhood. The word 'shift' was used, meaning petticoat, and the comic treatment of apparent patricide was an offence. The author had seen the repression and puritanism of his fellow Irishmen and women all too clearly. American Irish responded in the same way.

The very finest plays in English from the British Isles, even finer than the best of Shaw's, in the first half of our century are surely those of Sean O'Casey. He was born into a Protestant family in an Irish slum in 1880, and was a self-educated champion of the working class and a genius. His prose at its finest matches Shakespeare's. Though he wrote other plays, his claim to immortality is based on *Shadow of a Gunman* (1923), *Juno and the Paycock* (1924) and *The Plough and the Stars* (1926). All are set in the Dublin of the 'Troubles' (1916–22). There had been nothing like them since Jacobean England. They are tragedies of the highest rank, especially the second and third, but interspersed with comedy and even farce. Their prose is deeply poetic, realistic and unforgettable.

The last of the trio produced a riot, provoking the great poet Yeats to cry out: 'You have disgraced yourselves again' at the baying audience.

In 1928 O'Casey wrote his last great play, *The Silver Tassie*. It is a fine anti-war drama with a symbolic second act. The Abbey Theatre rejected it and O'Casey ceased writing for it. Charles Laughton, one of the finest British actors between the wars, not given to the excesses of some of his film performances, played the lead in London. O'Casey's later plays include *Red Roses for Me* and *Purple Dust*.

Whether *Juno* or *The Plough and the Stars* is the greater is a matter for the individual. It is typical of genius on a Shakespearean level that one of the most moving speeches in *Juno* is given to a minor part, a neighbour mourning her dead son, while the irony of the ending is unequalled in modern drama.

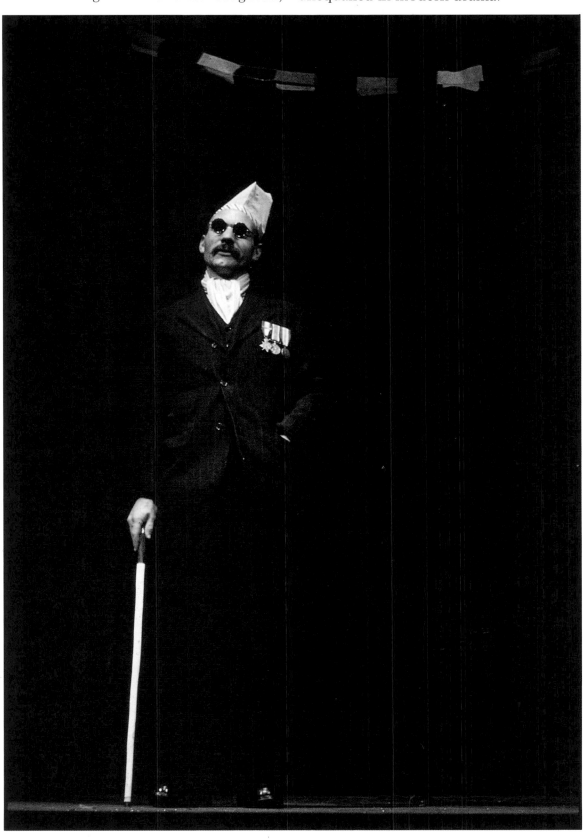

Left: Sean O'Casey's powerful The Silver Tassie *was revived by the Royal Shakespeare Company in 1969, Richard Moore playing the part created by Charles Laughton.*

Back to Britain

The arts boomed in the Second World War, including the commercial theatre. It was decided to bring the Old Vic Company back to life, and back it came at the New Theatre in 1944, the original building having been badly damaged in an air raid, with Olivier and Richardson, both released from the Fleet Air Arm, running the company with John Burrell. *Peer Gynt* opened the season with Richardson as Peer and Tyrone Guthrie as director. The third production was *Richard III*, the first appearance of Olivier as Richard, one of the legendary nights of theatre history. Great acting in the Kean and Irving tradition came back to London, the idea of it having been kept

alive by Gielgud, Donald Wolfit and a handful of others. Olivier presented a sardonic Satan rampant from his first deadly attractive spider of an entrance to his trapped, writhing dance of death at the end.

Glorious seasons followed. Richardson's Uncle Vanya was a triumph, so were Olivier's Hotspur and hilarious Justice Shallow. Guinness was the best Fool in *Lear* in living memory, and Margaret Leighton, Joyce Redman and Harry Andrews were among those who made their names. Then, in 1950, Richardson, Burrell and Olivier were sacked by the Vic's administrator, Llewellyn Rees, apparently and insultingly being considered to be mainly interested in their own careers.

Above: A scene from
Twelfth Night *at the Old*
Vic in 1950, with Peggy
Ashcroft as Viola, Robert
Eddison open-mouthed as
Sir Andrew and Roger
Livesey as an astounded
Sir Toby.

Olivier heard the news in Australia where he was with an Old Vic Company! The fine Old Vic School came to an end and such key figures as Michel St. Denis, George Devine and Glen Byam Shaw found themselves not wanted. The purge has never been properly explained. Rees seems not to have believed in the actors' dedication to the Vic. Fortunately, Hugh Hunt, Guthrie, Michael Benthall, Douglas Seale and, finally, Michael Elliot kept the Old Vic alive and standards high, a return to the old theatre being made in 1950. Richard Burton, John Neville and Robert Hardy were three of the actors who greatly enhanced their reputations at the Old Vic. Two productions of *Romeo and Juliet* stand out: one directed by Hugh Hunt with Alan Badel and Claire Bloom and another directed by Franco Zeffirelli in 1959 with John Stride and Judi Dench.

In a period when the West End was giving much undemanding pleasure there was great dissatisfaction because plays on certain subjects could not be staged in the commercial theatre. The trouble was the dreaded Lord Chamberlain, to whom playwrights had to submit their plays for approval, especially of sexual material and language. His rule went back to the eighteenth century when his concerns were mainly political and religious. (A full account can be read in Richard Findlater's *Banned*.)

Club theatres were particularly important, for at least members of them could see a number of important plays that would never be staged in the commercial theatre. The most famous such theatre was the Arts, until the English Stage Company at the Royal Court was founded in 1956. Earlier important clubs included The Repertory Players, the Everyman, the Mercury and the Gate, this last having been founded by Peter Godfrey, who staged the banned *Desire Under the Elms* by Eugene O'Neill in his 1930–31 season with Eric Portman and Flora Robson.

The club theatre could not get away with anything, however. On the contrary, Peter Cotes, the actor-director, was in constant conflict with the Lord

Overleaf: Pamela Brown,
Richard Burton and John
Gielgud in Christopher
Fry's verse comedy, The
Lady's Not For Burning,
a huge success in 1949.

175

Above: Joan Miller and Roger Moore in F. Tennyson Jesse's A Pin to See the Peepshow, *directed by Peter Cotes at the Playhouse, New York, in 1953. Banned from the West End by the Lord Chamberlain, this fine play was staged at the New Boltons, a club theatre.*

Censorship by the Lord Chamberlain was abolished in 1968 although plays are still subject to relevant laws. *Early Morning*, with Queen Victoria the gruff lover of Florence Nightingale, was the last play to be banned by the Lord Chamberlain. It hardly deserved the honour.

No account of the late 1940s and early 1950s can be complete without mentioning two popular authors of those days, the Englishman Christopher Fry and the Frenchman Jean Anouilh. Out of fashion in the 1980s, Fry's *The Lady's Not For Burning*, a spring-like enchantment of a medieval play, delighted all those who did not object to lack of dramatic impetus, and had a cast led by Gielgud and Pamela Brown, with the young Richard Burton and Claire Bloom playing what used to be called the juvenile leads. Fry usually had strong casts: his next play, *Venus Observed*, starred Olivier, with strong support from Denholm Elliott and others. He also translated plays by Giraudoux and Anouilh. The latter had many successes in Britain although he was not widely popular in France. His theme was often innocence lost by experience, his plays divided into *pièces noires*, *pièces brillantes*, *pièces roses* and *pièces grinçantes* (grating). Among them are *Antigone* (black), *The Waltz of the Toreadors* (grating) and *The Lark*, about Joan of Arc. Actors and audiences loved him. Some critics did.

This was a period of intimate revues, which needed very West End audiences to spot all the topical jokes and allusions. Dora Bryan, Ian Carmichael and Kenneth Williams became stars through such shows. Pre-1939 revues, with audiences in evening dress on the first and often other nights, had four supreme stars, Noël Coward, Gertrude Lawrence, Jack Buchanan and Beatrice Lillie, all equally at home in New York as well as London. Old-style revue in Britain died on the night Peter Cook, Jonathan Miller, Dudley Moore and Alan Bennett opened in *Beyond the Fringe* in 1960. Earlier, one-woman revues by Ruth Draper and Joyce Grenfell had been hugely successful. Perhaps the epitome of the revue artist was the wickedly witty Hermione Gingold.

American musicals made a great impact on Britain from the first night of *Oklahoma!* in 1947 and the opening of *Annie Get Your Gun* a few weeks later. Ten dazzling years ended with two more

Chamberlain. He had had a long career as an actor and director when he took over the New Lindsey Theatre in 1946. He won his first battle with the censor when *Pick-Up Girl* by Elsa Shelley was not only transferred to the West End, but also publicly enjoyed by that pillar of respectability, Queen Mary. Later, at the New Boltons, which became a most important theatre under him, he staged a number of fine modern plays, including two famous banned ones, Lillian Hellman's *The Children's Hour* and *A Pin to See the Peepshow* by H. M. Harwood and F. Tennyson Jesse. The first is a distinguished play about gossip and rumours of lesbianism between two teachers, the second a dramatization of the famous 1920s Thompson-Bywaters murder case. The case against the censor was helped by the fact that Cotes was a very fine director and that his wife, Joan Miller, was such an excellent and powerful actress that their theatre became a talking point.

stunning shows, *My Fair Lady* and *West Side Story*, the only snag being that the former's presenter, H. M. Tennent, managed to get a total ban on performances of Shaw's *Pygmalion*, on which the show is based, for the duration of the run. Those were the days when the shrewd and tough 'Binkie' Beaumont of Tennent's was as powerful as an absolute monarch in the West End, or so it was alleged, though his enemies would say as a Borgia.

America

In the early years of the twentieth century nothing it seemed could halt the progress of the American theatre except, briefly, in earthquake-stricken San Francisco. There were some 2,000 stock companies on the road by 1910 changing the bill nightly. There were also vast numbers of road shows, the most popular inevitably being those with Broadway stars in them. A crisis occurred when a tough theatre syndicate managed to corral most of the

nation's theatres. Eugene O'Neill's father was one of those who stood up to them, playing in tents or sports arenas rather than give in. Bernhardt and others did so, too, including the playwright Belasco, and the monopoly was finally broken.

Vaudeville

The famous Shubert Brothers came on the scene and fortunes were made by stars and producers alike in the theatre and booming vaudeville. Yet those low down the salary scale fell on harder times than usual. The American branch of the actors' trade union Equity called a strike in 1919, and stars as well as the lowly paid joined in the battle, all but a few, most notably, as Howard Tubman put it, 'the charm boy George M. Cohan'. The bosses gave in and there would not be another strike – a short one – until 1964.

The first vaudeville team to become stars were Joe Weber and Lew Fields, both child performers, who had a slapstick Dutch act, with Fields as the tall,

Above: The intimate revue, Sweet and Low (1943) with the astoundingly unique Hermione Gingold reclining. That fine actress Brenda Bruce looks amazed.

cunning one and Weber the small innocent. They had their own theatre in New York on Twenty-ninth Street from 1895 to 1904. Bert Williams was a major black star who appeared in eight editions of the *Ziegfeld Follies*. He was an under-player, who did not go in for endless eye-rolling.

Florenz Ziegfeld, born in 1867, was a consummate master of costly, ultra glamorous shows, with wildly expensive costumes for his casts. His *Follies* outlived him, running from 1907 to 1957, the great impresario dying in 1932. His stated object was 'Glorifying the American girl', while talents he helped to thrive included W. C. Fields, Eddie Cantor and, among his Girls, Irene Dunne, Marion Davies, Barbara Stanwyck and Paulette Goddard. His judgement was as superb as his flair and, like his shows, he was an American institution. He also staged straight plays and musicals, including *Show Boat*.

Will Rogers, the part-Indian who graduated from Wild West shows to become 'the world's number one wisecracker', became a horse-and-lariat performer in vaudeville in 1905. He later became best known for his comments on world and local events and assorted enemies of his, including Republicans, bankers and lawyers. He used all the media of his day, his wisecracks were repeated by countless fans, and he became a Hollywood star – and a lecturer, radio commentator and journalist.

W. C. Fields, born in 1880, mercifully made enough films for us to experience his genius. He joined Ziegfeld in 1916, speaking for the first time, having started as a juggler, then a silent tramp juggler, an act that conquered Parisians at the Folies-Bergère as well as his fellow Americans. The famous bulbous nose came from early fights, the voice from ill-health, the monstrous, pessimistic grandeur, the superb timing, the marvellous Micawber in *David Copperfield*, being left to us in his movies. Vaudeville gave Hollywood supreme talents: the Marx Brothers; Jimmy Durante; Eddie Cantor; the Liverpool-born master of the one-liner, Henry Youngman; Jack Benny; Mae West, whose first play was called *Sex*; Burns and Allen; Danny Kaye; Bob Hope; Milton Berle; George Jessel, appointed by President Truman to be Toastmaster General of the United States; and Bert Lahr, a famous Broadway comedian long before his immortal Cowardly Lion in

Opposite: W.C. Fields
doing his superb act in the
1920s before settling in
Hollywood.

Left: The great Jimmy
Durante in Jumbo at the
Hippodrome, New York in
1935, staged by Billy Rose.

Below: Bert Lahr regally
splendid as Queen
Victoria in Two on the
Aisle, a revue at the Mark
Hellinger.

The Wizard of Oz. He was a major star, who also played one of the tramps in Waiting for Godot in 1956. And to end this all-too-short list, there was Fanny Brice, whose career inspired Funny Girl, in which Barbra Streisand played her. She was a mimic, a singer of dialect songs who could brilliantly burlesque ballet and modern dance, Martha Graham included. She was in her forties when she had her greatest success, in the Ziegfeld Follies of 1934, which the Shuberts staged after the great man had died. There was also Al Jolson, who, through no fault of his own, helped to destroy vaudeville when he started to sing on screen.

Coming of age

Playwrights of the highest quality were naturally, as always, in shorter supply, but this was the era when America's greatest dramatist was writing.

Eugene O'Neill (1888–1953) was the son of James O'Neill, the James Tyrone of Long Day's Journey into Night. As the play recalls, the father opted out of following in the footsteps of the great Edwin Booth by choosing to immur himself in 'that play', The Count of Monte Cristo. He played the lead more than 6,000 times from 1883 until 1891, later playing it again.

His son worked in business, became a sailor, then a reporter. His health broke down and he was in a sanitorium for a spell. There he began to write a play called The Web. When he emerged he attended

181

one of Professor George Baker's courses in drama at Harvard, then worked with the Provincetown Players who, in conjunction with the Greenwich Village Players, would present some of his early works. Success came with his first full-length play, *Beyond the Horizon* in 1920. It is set in rural New England, and is more realistic than most plays of the day. Two short plays were followed by *The Emperor Jones* (1925), later seen in London, where Paul Robeson would play the title-role first taken by Charles Gilpin.

There followed 14 very productive years. *Anna Christie* (1921), with a 'fallen' daughter redeemed by love, and the dramatist criticized for a happy ending, is a fine play set in a saloon. *Gold*, *The First Man* and *All God's Chillun Got Wings* and others followed, also *The Hairy Ape*, staged by the Provincetown Players in 1922. He was accused of copying the German expressionists, as he had been in *The Emperor Jones*, but denied having seen

Below: Eugene O'Neill, America's greatest dramatist.

any of that genre. The 'Ape' is an ox-like worker below decks in a ship, the heroine seeking kicks among the lower orders on the lowest decks. It is strong, viable drama. *All God's Chillun* is a despairing piece about a mixed marriage, and in the same year, 1924, came *Desire Under the Elms*, with the great Walter Huston bringing a young wife home to a New England farm in the 1850s, an idyll being destroyed by incest and greed. The police were called in, but the show went on.

The Great God Brown in 1926 was his greatest play to date in some opinions, a dual study of relationships in a family and between a man and his soul. It is a prostitute, not the wife, who sees the

artist's frightened sensitivity. *Marco's Millions* (1928) is an attack on materialism, and the same year came the vast, powerful *Strange Interlude* with Lynn Fontanne in the lead. Despite its Wagnerian length, it created a stir, portraying the inner and exterior personalities of two people.

Mourning Becomes Electra (1931) is again very long, an *Oresteia* set in New England after the American civil war. It lacks, according to its creator, great language, but these three plays in one, originally with Alice Brady as an Electra-like figure, and Nazimova, Clytemnestra, made and make a powerful impression. In contrast *Ah, Wilderness!* is a pleasing and personal

nostalgic comedy in which the playwright relived a happy part of his youth.

O'Neill's next play, *Days without End* (1934), failed and he retired to brood and to create a whole series of plays. He returned with *The Iceman Cometh* (1946). (Kenneth Tynan commented later that O'Neill wrote clumsily and top-heavily but spoke of his autobiographical intensity. Tynan felt in the presence of a man 'whose vision of life is as profoundly dark as any since Aeschylus'.) The last play produced in his lifetime was *A Moon for the Misbegotten* (1947), successfully staged in New York and London.

O'Neill's masterpiece was staged long after his death, the great *Long Day's*

Above: Susan Tracy as Eugene O'Neill's Anna Christie, staged at the Warehouse Theatre by the Royal Shakespeare Company in 1979.

Right: Olivier's towering James Tyrone in Long Day's Journey into Night, *directed by Michael Blakemore for the National Theatre at the Old Vic.*

Journey into Night, a major performance of which is a landmark in a theatregoer's experience: so the National Theatre's production by Michael Elliott with Olivier in the lead in 1972 would suggest. O'Neill's alleged poverty of language, his cliché-ridden dialogue, are often cited, but the play acts better than it reads. It is a 'play of old sorrow written in tears and blood' about his own family. His sweet, drug-addict mother is wonderfully drawn, and O'Neill himself is Edmund. The failed wastrel Jamie is his elder brother whom he hates as well as loves.

The play is extremely long, brutal and sublime, with rare moments of humour. The much-criticized lack of poetic flair must be set against short effective Anglo-Saxon monosyllables that when needed become stab wounds. What theatregoer can ever forget the great scene in which Tyrone reveals himself to his son and says: 'It was in those days that I learnt to be a miser.' As for the play's last line, at the climax of what is a mad scene, the mother says: 'I fell in love with James Tyrone and was so happy for a time.' Then the curtain falls on long years of love, blame, and torment and hate unleashed in one terrible, awe-full day and night. Frederick Marsh, Florence Eldridge, Jason Robards and Bradford Dillman (Edmund) were the original cast, directed by José Quintero.

Long before his masterpiece was revealed in New York and Stockholm in 1956, the American Theatre had come of age. The work of the Civic Repertory Theater (1926–33) is a landmark. It was founded by the London-born actress, producer and director Eva Le Galliene, who presented and acted in major American and foreign plays, giving over 1,500 performances from Shakespeare and Chekhov to Dumas in a 'huge decrepit barn of a house on West 14th Street', wrote Howard Taubman. Salaries were only a little larger than those offered by Lilian Baylis. In the 1950s she tried again aided by Margaret Webster and Cheryl Crawford. The bold venture failed because the trades unions wanted full complements of stagehands even for small-cast plays, and because the public was suspicious of plays in repertory.

Back in the 1920s Maxwell Anderson (1888–1959) had begun producing comedies, historical plays and social criticism, even verse dramas. He was a skilled theatre craftsman. His greatest successes after writing the American First

World War play, *What Price Glory?*, in 1924 were *Mary of Scotland*, *Winterset*, which dealt with the notorious Sacco-Vanzetti case, *Key Largo*, also a famous film, and the splendidly melodramatic *The Bad Seed*.

George Kaufman (1889–1961), 'the great collaborator', was a true man of the theatre and a very fine director. Moss Hart wrote a brilliant portrait of him in

Below: Humphrey Bogart and Ruth Gordon in Saturday's Children *on Broadway in 1928. This was Ruth Gordon's first great success.*

Act I. Among his successes were *Dulcy*, *Merton of the Movies* and *Beggar on Horseback*, with Marc Connelly. *The Royal Family* was about the Barrymores, and, like *Dinner at Eight* and *Stage Door*, were with Edna Furber. He won the annual Pulitzer Prize for drama with *You Can't Take it With You*, written with Moss Hart, and *The Man Who Came to Dinner*. He was a first-rate director of other people's shows and a great figure on Broadway. There was also Charles MacArthur, who wrote the best of all newspaper plays, *Front Page*, with Ben Hecht, who collaborated with him again in *Twentieth Century*.

Elmer Rice (1892–1967) attacked regimented materialism in his finest play, *The Adding Machine* (1923) and won a Pulitzer Prize with *Street Scene* – sentiment-cum-violence. *Judgement Day* is strongly anti-Nazi. His contemporary S. N. Behrman (1893–1973) is considered by many the finest native playwright of the comedy of manners. His successes include *No Time for Comedy*.

The anti-naturalist Thornton Wilder (1897–1975) was also a noted novelist. He made his theatrical name with *Our Town* in which he very successfully conveys a small community, using the stage manager as guide. *The Merchant of Yonkers* (1938) later became *The Matchmaker*, then *Hello Dolly!*, a trio of delights, while his comic strip history of the world, *The Skin of Your Teeth*, triumphed on both sides of the Atlantic. Like *Our Town* it won a Pulitzer.

The best known play of Lillian Hellman (born in 1905) is *The Children's Hour* (1934). It had a tremendous success on Broadway, but its theme of lesbianism got it banned in Britain. This fine play was followed by *The Little Foxes*, also a Bette Davis film, *The Watch on the Rhine*, *Another Part of the Forest* and a torrid Southern drama, *Toys in the Attic*.

Clifford Odets (1906–63) was a most influential figure, too little known in Britain except for *The Country Girl*, renamed *Winter Journey* in the West End. It is a much underrated (in Britain), magnificently theatrical backstage story. With Harold Clurman, Cheryl Crawford and Lee Strasberg, Odets had founded the Group Theatre in 1931. The company included Stella and Luther Adler, Franchot Tone, Morris Carnovsky – later a magnificent King Lear – John Garfield, Elia Kazan and J. Edward Bromberg. As well as Odets, the group's playwrights

included Robery Ardrey, William Saroyan, Sidney Kingsley and Irwin Shaw. This extremely gifted team lasted a decade.

Odets' *Waiting for Lefty* had an extraordinary effect on its audiences on both sides of the Atlantic. In New York it seemed a virtual summons to arms. Based on a New York taxi drivers' strike, it has six scenes, most related to the workers' meeting. Scenes include two bleak views of home life, an interview between a lab

Left: Thornton Wilder's brilliant The Skin of Our Teeth *gave Vivien Leigh as Sabina one of her best roles. Tallulah Bankhead had created the part on Broadway.*

assistant and a poison gas maker, a spy being found at the workers' meeting, an actor trying for a job, and two doctors, one a Jew, in which American medical practice is attacked. It can no longer have the impact it once had, but at its best, its humanity, impact and fire make parts of it dateless. It is American conscience drama at its most potent. Odets also wrote *Wake and Sing*, a portrait of a Jewish working class boy. *Golden Boy*, the portrait of a young violinist ruined by being forced to box, gave him and the Group a commercial success. *Till The Day I Die* was anti-Nazi, *The Big Knife* very anti-Hollywood.

The Federal Theater Project was a scheme begun in 1935 during the Depression, indirectly inspired by President Roosevelt's New Deal for National Recovery. It helped give over 10,000 theatre people work, half of them in New York. It was directed by Hallie Flanagan, who was accused of being a

communist, and soon collapsed with the banning of some of the productions. It had produced more than 1,000 plays, amateur, professional, traditional and experimental ones, also opera, ballet and puppets shows. The Living Newspaper, started by Elmer Rice, was a series of productions about current topics, while Orson Welles and John Houseman created memorable productions: a black *Macbeth*, *Doctor Faustus* and *The Cradle Will Rock*, Marc Blitzstein's anti-capitalist opera. *It Can't Happen Here*, a broadside against local fascism, had 21 premières in different cities at the same time. In 1939 it was abolished by political pressure.

Orson Welles and John Houseman then opened their famous Mercury Theater on Broadway, starting with an anti-fascist modern dress *Julius Caesar* – who looked liked Mussolini, while Brutus became a feeble liberal, an idea copied since. The venture included *Heartbreak House*, *Danton's Death* and *The Shoemaker's Holiday*, a splendid trio. Welles's parts included Brutus and Shotover in *Heartbreak House*. Casts included George Colouris, Vincent Price, Joseph Cotten and Frederic Tozere. The group frightened the nation – literally – with their modern radio version of *The War of the Worlds*, which people believed to be true and therefore fled in panic. A short, glorious, merry time was had by all. *Citizen Kane* soon followed.

The Romanian-born, English-educated Houseman later saved the Shakespeare Festival at Stratford, Connecticut, from 'chronic provincialism' in the 1950s, so wrote the critic Brooks Atkinson. His wide-ranging career includes striking appearances in films.

Broadway and beyond

Meanwhile, between the world wars, Broadway, like the West End, was more concerned with entertainment than with conscience dramas, and there were wonderful stars to entertain its audiences. Most stellar of all, John Barrymore (1882–1942), was an undisciplined actor who from time to time showed himself to be a genius. His father was Maurice Barrymore. Born in Britain, and Cambridge educated, he crossed the Atlantic in the 1870s and was much in demand as a handsome leading man. His eldest child was Ethel Barrymore, whose career ranged from acting with Irving in *The Bells* to being a magnificent Miss Moffat in Emlyn Williams's *The Corn is Green*. The oldest Barrymore was Lionel, best remembered for his film roles. John Barrymore, the youngest, had a famous profile, great talent and a genius for living it up. A notable Richard III, he is best remembered in the theatre – he made a number of films – as Hamlet, in New York in 1922 and in London in 1925. He had first made his name in Galsworthy's *Justice* as a cockney bank clerk.

His Hamlet ranks with Forbes-Robertson's and John Gielgud's as the most famous of the century, 'the realest Hamlet' as the critic Alexander Woollcott noted. He made history by playing his scene with his mother as a love scene. He was poetic, witty, energetic, graceful, fiery and beautifully spoken. His Laertes in London had to be changed several times as Barrymore fought so realistically. He then abandoned the theatre, classical and modern, contributing to the death of a classical tradition on the American stage.

Always loyal to the stage were Alfred Lunt and his English-born wife Lynn Fontanne who, from the time of their marriage in 1922, acted together, displaying a technique that was the delight and despair of professionals and the joy of audiences. They excelled in Coward, Berhman and Robert Sherwood, whose plays included *There Shall be No Night*, *Idiot's Delight* and *Reunion in Vienna* with them, also *The Petrified Forest*, a gangster drama, *Abe Lincoln in Illinois* and *Waterloo Bridge*, better known as a film.

The Lunts also did serious plays for The Theater Guild, which had been founded in 1918 to present fine plays not guaranteed to be commercially viable. Brooks Atkinson called the Guild the

John and Ethel Barrymore in Barrie's A Slice of Life. *This is the first picture of them acting together.*

most enlightened and influential theatre organization that New York ever enjoyed. Alfred Lunt was a fine director, and Broadway's only outright male star in an era dominated by women. Lynn Fontanne was regarded by Brooks Atkinson and others as the finest of all Eliza Doolittles.

Katherine Cornell (1898–1974) was at the height of her fame between the world wars. Her most famous role was Elizabeth Barrett in *The Barretts of Wimpole Street*, and she was also a very fine Candida. At the height of the Depression she toured 75,000 miles with these two roles, also acting Juliet. Her husband, Guthrie McClintic, regularly directed her.

Helen Hayes, born in 1900, was considered the finest actress of her day by many theatregoers. She was adept at playing queens, Shaw's Cleopatra, Mary in Maxwell Anderson's *Mary of Scotland*, and – according to Brooks Atkinson – her masterpiece, Victoria in *Victoria Regina*. Another great success was in Barrie's *What Every Woman Knows*. She made her Broadway debut aged nine.

Tallulah Bankhead was more personality than actress in the 1920s when she was London's darling, very beautiful and outrageous. The critic J. C. Trewin has written of the smoky huskiness of her voice. A player of many a femme fatale, she was a superb Julia in Coward's *Fallen Angels*, but her notices for Cleopatra – which she used to read out publicly – were appalling, including John Mason Brown's: 'Miss Bankhead barged down the Nile last night – and sank.'

The post-war years

Very different is Jessica Tandy. British-born, she was the first Blanche in Tennessee Williams's *A Streetcar Named Desire* (1949), winning major awards. She has played major roles at the Old Vic, Stratford, Connecticut, and the Tyrone Guthrie at Minneapolis. With her actor husband Hume Cronyn she spent, it has been calculated, more time in bed than any other stage couple – two years on Broadway and on tour in Jan de Hartog's *The Fourposter*.

That much-admired actress, Katherine Hepburn, got off to a slow start, the most blazing example of it being Dorothy Parker's comment on an early performance that she 'ran the whole gamut of emotion from A to B'. Her many successes have included Shaw's *The Millionairess* in London and New York in 1952.

Above: Lynn Fontanne and Alfred Lunt in 1929. They acted together to perfection.

Right: Helen Hayes in Mrs McThing. *She excelled in most roles especially playing queens. She was the first Amanda in Tennessee Williams's* The Glass Menagerie *and was outstanding in O'Neill's* A Touch of the Poet.

Opposite: Vivien Leigh as Blanche du Bois in A Streetcar Named Desire *in 1949, one of her finest roles.*

Overleaf: Arthur Miller's magnificent All My Sons *was revived in London in 1981 with Colin Blakely and Rosemary Harris as the father and mother.*

Marlon Brando had a brief, exhilarating career on the stage, securing a place in theatre history with his Stanley in *A Streetcar Named Desire* in 1947. This brings us to the careers of two most notable playwrights of the twentieth century.

Tennessee Williams (1911–83) had his first success with *The Glass Menagerie* in 1945, a wistful autobiographical play, a 'memory' play, of considerable charm. Next in order of production (1947) was his most famous play, *A Streetcar Named Desire*, which proclaimed a major – a searing – talent and also great lyrical gifts. *Summer and Smoke*, with a theme of loneliness, followed, complete with the playwright's 'eternally baleful female', as Taubman put it. *The Rose Tattoo*, *Camino Real* and *Cat on a Hot Tin Roof* appeared between 1951–55. Most of his plays were heavily bowdlerized when turned into films: *Orpheus Descending*, *Suddenly Last Summer*, a horrifying play, and *Sweet Bird of Youth* which has a threatened castration as its climax, but Paul Newman in the film merely has his nose broken.

The sultry, eerie *Night of the Iguana* is possibly the finest of the later plays, though *Small Craft Warnings* (1972) showed the old mastery. Lyrical, sensuous, sometimes savage, almost always atmospheric, Tennessee Williams at his finest is a great playwright. When he repels, he still remains hypnotic.

His fellow master of his craft was Arthur Miller, and may be again. Born in 1915, Miller was brought up in the Depression. His work reveals a strong social concern, with an abiding interest in the family and its relationships, also the responsibilities that come with it. *All My Sons* (1947) was his first major success, with a family facing the facts of war profiteering and individual guilt. Then came a masterpiece, *Death of a Salesman* (1948), with its pitiful hero, Willy Loman, played by Lee J. Cobb. Each character is memorable, and the playwright makes Willy, essentially a little man, sorry for himself, into a tragic figure. Miller's adaptation of Ibsen's *An Enemy of the People* flopped for reasons that can only reflect badly on the Broadway of the day, but *The Crucible*, a modern reworking of the Salem witch trials, was successful. There followed *A View from the Bridge* and other plays, notably *The Price* (1968), which was much more admired in London than New York where it was suddenly fashionable to despise family

Right: Geraldine Page and Paul Newman in Sweet Bird of Youth *by Tennessee Williams. She was voted Best Actress of the Year by the New York critics for her performance.*

Right: Arthur Miller's masterpiece, Death of a Salesman. *Left to right, Mildred Dunnock, Lee J. Cobb as Willy Loman, Arthur Kennedy and Cameron Mitchell.*

dramas, political subjects being in vogue. *After the Fall* (1964), inspired by the playwright's marriage to Marilyn Monroe, was perhaps staged too soon. Other plays include *Incident at Vichy* (1968), a searing look at the way the persecution of the Jews could happen. Even if he writes no more plays Miller's place in the history of drama is secure. Meanwhile, playgoers can only lament his absence and the critical attacks on him at a crucial period.

The controversial technique of Method acting stemmed from what seems to its opponents to be a misunderstanding of Stanislavsky. It came into prominence thanks to the Actors' Studio, started by Elia Kazan in 1947. Lee Strasberg became director in 1951. It claimed that only by exploring a character personally can an actor reach the truth. Too many actors became so self-absorbed that they and their colleagues suffered, while it could have fatal results in classical plays. Brando, Dean and other major talents have used the Method to advantage in *films* – with their many 'takes' – but the stage is a different matter. Burl Ives told graphically what could happen. When acting downstage in a Tennessee Williams play, a youthful Method actor vanished

Left: *Ella Snyder as The Bowery Girl of* The Belle of New York.

upstage and started mixing drinks, a great distraction from what Ives was saying. When he taxed the young hopeful, the scene wrecker replied: 'I was making a life for myself on stage.' It is one thing to explore a part and, as the Actors' Studio instituted, criticize each other, another to get across to an audience in the right way. Strasberg's *The Three Sisters* in London in 1965 was much criticized.

The musical

The most notable product of Broadway in modern times has been the musical. The word has been for several decades a blanket term for musical comedies, musical dramas, folk operas, operettas and so on.

In America the first musical is usually reckoned to be *The Black Crook* of 1866. It was a strong melodrama with ballet and songs which, despite its five hours, was a huge success. The great age of musical comedy followed, with (usually) thin plots, but with fine settings, song, dance and humour. In London there was a master in charge at the Gaiety Theatre, the legendary George Edwardes, and titles included *A Gaiety Girl*, *The Quaker Girl* and *A Country Girl*, some tunes from which are still heard on the radio. *The Belle of New York* by Gustave Kerker is a famous American example of the genre, first seen in London in 1898. Leslie Stuart's *Floradora* and Lionel Monkton's *The Arcadians* are also remembered while the American Victor Herbert (1859–1924) wrote popular operettas and ranks as Broadway's first great composer of musicals, with *Naughty Marietta* one of his most famous. None equalled Lehár, whose *The Merry Widow* is virtually a classical piece now, as are the operettas of Offenbach.

Tuneful, sentimental, romantic hokum was provided by two masters, Sigmund (*The Desert Song*, *The New Moon*, *The Student Prince*) Romberg, at the height of his powers in the 1920s, and Rudolf (*Rose Marie*, *The Vagabond King*) Friml, who was in action at the same period. *Rose Marie* was the first American musical to dominate Drury Lane in the mid-1920s, a domination that would last until Ivor Novello in the 1930s. It ran for 557 performances on Broadway and 851 at Drury Lane theatre, remarkable runs for those times.

The first great breakthrough was *Show Boat* (1927), with its incomparable score by Jerome Kern and its fusion of music and drama. The very opening, with a gang of black dock workers, made history: usually a high-stepping chorus line started the proceedings. Oscar Hammerstein wrote the book from Edna Ferber's novel and the lyrics. In 1928 Paul Robeson was the definitive Joe at Drury Lane.

Other landmarks included Gershwin's near-operatic masterpiece, *Of Thee I Sing* (1931). His brother Ira provided the lyrics for this political satire. Another step forward was *Pal Joey* (1940) by Richard Rodgers and Lorenz Hart, though it ran longer at its 1952 revival. Rodgers later noted that it forced the entire musical comedy theatre to wear long pants for the first time. This was the show that made Gene Kelly a star.

There were legendary musicals before *Oklahoma!* among them Gershwin's *Lady, Be Good*, and his folk opera, now regarded as an opera period piece, *Porgy and Bess* (1935). Lorenz Hart wrote the most witty and skilful lyrics between the wars, collaborating with Richard Rodgers in *On Your Toes*, *Babes in Arms* and *The Boys from Syracuse*. The great comedian Bert Lahr starred in many musicals, his classic performance being in *Du Barry Was a Lady*, moving the critic Richard Watts to write that he acted with a sort of 'spluttering violence and leering impudence that makes him one of the best comedians in the world'.

Oklahoma!, which opened in 1943 in New York, was the *Tamburlaine*, the *Rigoletto*, of the modern musical as a major art form. It blended as never before music, dancing and a strong story line

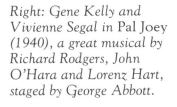

Right: Gene Kelly and Vivienne Segal in Pal Joey *(1940), a great musical by Richard Rodgers, John O'Hara and Lorenz Hart, staged by George Abbott.*

into an enchanting and very American whole. For Richard Rodgers and Oscar Hammerstein, both exceptionally talented men of the musical theatre, *Oklahoma!* proved to be the start of a long partnership. They had Reuben Mamoulian as their director and Agnes de Mille as choreographer. The show ran for 2,248 performances. Drury Lane housed it in 1947 for 1,543 performances. The first night is theatre legend. The pair would write greater shows perhaps, but *Oklahoma!* remains the landmark musical. *Carousel* is their finest show musically if not dramatically, *South Pacific* surely their masterpiece (1949). In New York it starred two talents who were indeed towering: Mary Martin, who had become a star back in 1938 when she sang 'My Heart Belongs to Daddy' in *Leave It To Me*, removing ermine wraps and singing in a baby voice the while, and the great operatic bass with a personality to match, Ezio Pinza. London, with a less stupendous cast, was enchanted with the show from 1951. *The King and I*, starring

Gertrude Lawrence and Yul Brynner, opened in 1951, showed only a slight decline, then in 1959 came *The Sound of Music*. For all its charm and great commercial success, it is not to be compared with the pair's finest pieces.

Other glorious shows in this stellar period included Irving Berlin's masterpiece *Annie Get Your Gun* (1946) with a steady stream of hit songs, with the trumpet-toned Ethel Merman as sharpshooting Annie Oakley of Buffalo Bill's Wild West Show in New York. London had a superb Annie also in Dolores Gray (1947).

In the same league as *Annie* was *Kiss Me, Kate*, inspired by *The Taming of the Shrew*, the book therefore by Sam and Bella Spewak and Shakespeare. The music and lyrics were a triumph for the great Cole Porter and the cast, directed by John C. Wilson, and led by Alfred Drake and Patricia Morrison, also triumphed. The glorious score helped make it very popular in Europe, where opera and operetta companies stage it. Like so many

197

Below: The King and I by Rodgers and Hammerstein starred Gertrude Lawrence and made a star of Yul Brynner.

of the great musicals it was superbly filmed. Howard Keel played Curly in *Oklahoma!* in London as Harold Keel, starring there with Kathryn Grayson and Ann Miller.

In 1956 and 1957 the musical reached its twin peaks with the perfection of Lerner and Loewe's *My Fair Lady* and the revolutionary explosion of talent that produced *West Side Story*. The former, based on Shaw's *Pygmalion* very closely, is blessed by magnificent music and book. Alan Jay Lerner provided the book and lyrics, Frederick Loewe the music, the designer was Cecil Beaton and the choreographer Hanja Holm. Rex Harrison was a definitive Professor Higgins, Julie Andrews an excellent Eliza Doolittle, Stanley Holloway – as definitive as Harrison – as Doolittle. It reached the Theatre Royal Drury Lane in 1958 with the same trio.

West Side Story reworks *Romeo and Juliet*, placing the action in gangland New York, the Montagues becoming young native New Yorkers, the Capulets Puerto Rican immigrants, and demands perfection in all departments. This has usually been so in acting, always in dancing, but, except on the famous recording never quite reached the required standard in singing. José Carreras has proved the point with his incomparable performance. Jerome Robbins had the inspired idea for the show and was the director and choreographer, the truly great score, matching Robbins's achievement, is by Leonard Bernstein, Arthur Laurents wrote the book and Stephen Sondheim the lyrics. If Robbins had achieved nothing else – and his credits include *On The Town*, *Gypsy* and *Fiddler on the Roof* – he would still be regarded with awe.

Since these two great shows the American musical has owed more to Stephen Sondheim than anyone else. This composer-lyricist's credits include *A Funny Thing Happened on the Way to the*

Right: West Side Story has been a classic for so long that its original impact is not realized by the younger generation. Jerome Robbins masterminded the show, while Leonard Bernstein's music has also achieved classic status.

Opposite: Topol in a 1983 revival of the magnificent musical, Fiddler on the Roof, based on Tevye the Milkman by the Jewish writer, Sholom Aleichem.

198

Forum, Company, a scintillating and searing study of modern marriage, and his throwback to the Ziegfeld style, *Follies*, as well as *Merrily We Roll Roll Along*. His most remarkable achievement is *Sweeney Todd* (1979), which critic Michael Billington has noted as the first musical about cannabalism – based on the lurid melodrama of the demon barber of Fleet Street who turned his customers into meat pies.

One last American musical must be noted. *A Chorus Line* (1975), the inspired idea of Marvin Hamlish, is a virtually plotless show with dancers auditioning for parts and telling their life/career stories to the choreographer-director. It won a Pulitzer Prize. Michael Bennett masterminded the ultra-professional show.

Germany

Germany had a rich theatrical life in the late nineteenth and early twentieth centuries, until stifled by Hitler. Gerhart Hauptmann (1862–1946) succumbed to the blandishments of the Nazis, but his earlier career had been notable. *Die Weber* (The Weavers), 1892, portrayed a revolt of Silesian weavers in 1844, with the crowd as hero, a novelty that influenced later writers. His *Der Biberpelz* (The Beaver Coat) is a brilliant comedy, and he was also a master of fantasy and symbolism. His best work was done before the First World War, another notable piece being *Die Ratten* (The Rats) in 1911, a gloom-laden play set in a poor quarter of Berlin. He soon won a Nobel Prize.

Frank Wedekind, born two years after Hauptmann, was an actor and singer as well as a playwright. His constant theme is sex and its effects, his most famous play on the theme *Frühlings Erwachen* (Spring Awakening), an 1891 play banned in Britain in 1963! He made the world he created more real than that of the naturalists, for he went to the very heart of the human comedy and tragedy. Wedekind had a considerable influence on Bertolt Brecht. Germany also had a number of very fine actors. Albert Basserman, to be seen in Hollywood films after he left Germany because of Hitler,

Right: Stephen Sondheim's operatic musical, Sweeney Todd, *is arguably his masterpiece. Dennis Quilley and Sheila Hancock played the leads at Drury Lane.*

Left: Frank Wedekind's
Spring Awakening *was*
staged by the National
Theatre in 1974 with a
translation by Edward
Bond.

was with the Meininger company in the 1890s, then joined Otto Brahm's Deutsches Theater in Berlin, where he became Germany's most noted player of the great Ibsen roles. He was also renowned in Shakespeare, Schiller and Goethe. He worked regularly with Max Reinhardt, who took over the Deutsches Theater from Brahm, but Reinhardt was also forced to leave Germany, having master-minded the creation of the Salzburg Festival in 1920, regularly staging the morality play *Everyman* there. Few have done more to advance the power of the director, while few have ranged so widely in the theatre arts, Zeffirelli is his nearest modern equivalent.

He is best remembered for his lavish productions and his handling of crowds, his sets often vast and towering. Famous productions of his included *Oedipus Rex* in London in 1911, the same year as he staged *The Miracle* there. Some considered his work vulgar, others praised his popularizing genius. He collaborated with great painters and musicians and directed the famous film of *A Midsummer Night's Dream*, with James Cagney as a first-rate Bottom and Mickey Rooney as the definitive Puck.

Reinhardt made Berlin Europe's theatre capital. He more than anyone carried out the theories of Ellen Terry's son Gordon Craig on design, lighting and the stage. With Adolf Appia he broke with the realistic tradition in set design and lighting, indeed breaking with the orthodox proscenium theatre. He was therefore an early exponent of the arena theatre.

The playwrights George Kaiser and Ernst Toller pioneered Expressionism in the theatre between the wars. This was a reaction against realism and resulted in plays with unnamed characters – Man, Captain and so on. Spiritual renewal was what mattered, along with strong emotions. Detail did not matter. One of Toller's most notable works was *The Machine Wreckers* (1920), and Kaiser's key works were *Gas 1* and *Gas 2*. O'Neill, O'Casey (in *The Silver Tassie*) and the

Below: A scene from Max Reinhardt's production of A Midsummer Night's Dream *in the Boboli Gardens in Florence.*

Czechoslovak Capek (*The Insect Play*) were all influenced by Expressionism.

These playwrights were clearly worlds away from Reinhardt, but he had a disciple in Erwin Piscator (1893–1966). Piscator wanted 'epic' theatre, big plays that were political and episodic and determined to ram their messages home. He used film and non-realistic settings, and he influenced Bertholt Brecht, with whom he dramatized *The Good Soldier Schweik* in 1927. Piscator had a short spell as director of Moscow's International Theatre (1931–33), but worked mainly in New York and West Germany, directing a famous *War and Peace* there in 1951, and at the Bristol Old Vic in 1962.

Leading actors of the period in Germany included Werner Krauss, a magnificent Shakespearean who had made his name in Wedekind, and Gustaf

*Left: The National
Theatre's production of
Schweyk in the Second
World War by Brecht,
with Bill Paterson as
Schweyk.*

Gründgens, who was intendant at the Berlin National Theatre in 1935 and a notable player of Shakespeare and Shaw. He produced John Osborne's *The Entertainer* at Hamburg in 1957. The superb film *Mephisto*, about an actor who decides to collaborate with the Nazis, is inspired by Klaus Mann's novel about Gründgens.

The controversial Bertolt Brecht (1878–1956) took Piscator's ideas a stage further with his 'alienation effect'. For him the actor should not 'live' his part, but be outside it – while completely understanding it – enough to make a 'comment' on it. The audience meanwhile is expected to judge each character critically. Brecht meant this as a guide rather than as a rigid discipline. The result is the 'theatre of debate', his early plays proclaiming the advantages of commun-

ism. Meanwhile, his techniques included a narrator singing, slides, and lighting simply as illumination, not for effect. He founded his famous Berliner Ensemble in 1949 at the Deutsches Theater, East Berlin. The company's visits to London were a revolution in themselves, not because he turned British playwrights into hard line Brechtians – Brecht himself trimmed for the sake of theatre – but because his ideas were so exciting. Arden, Bolt, Osborne, Shaffer and Whiting are some of those he has influenced in varying degrees.

Brecht's first and one of his greatest was *The Threepenny Opera*, with a brilliant score by Kurt Weill. This anti-bourgeois updating of *The Beggar's Opera* was followed by the more powerful *The Rise and Fall of the City of Mahagonny* (1930), his masterpiece. He left Germany in 1933

Judi Dench as Brecht's indomitable Mother Courage.

and went to America, where he entered his finest period from 1937 to 1954: *The Life of Galileo, The Resistible Rise of Arturo Ui* – Hitler and his rise in terms of Al Capone's Chicago, a brilliant theatrical device – and *The Caucasian Chalk Circle*.

He went back to (East) Germany in 1949 and his reputation soared. The alienation effect he advocated has always been slightly suspect. *Mother Courage*, the anti-heroine, profiteer and survivor of the 30 Years' War is so sympathetically drawn, so indomitable, that alienation is hardly in evidence. For it must be stressed that Brecht was too much a man of the theatre to keep too rigidly to theories, which means that the best of his plays will survive. His wife was the famous Helene Weigel, herself a brilliant Mother Courage. Other leading German actors include Martin Held, a major classical performer who has also played Beckett

under the direction of the playwright, and Ekkehard Schall, who created many roles for the Berliner Ensemble, including Brecht's Coriolan, and a true star actor, the sort of fact of life Brecht had to face up to, and, indeed, doubtless accepted, whatever he publicly proclaimed.

France

It has been the French theatre's great good fortune that there have been some magnificent actresses since the age of Bernhardt. Marie Bell, born in 1900, excelled in the great classical roles at the Comédie-Française and also as Madame in Genet's *Le Balcon* (The Balcony). Maria Casarés, born in 1922, joined the great theatre in 1952 and has starred in Pirandello, Marivaux and Camus as well as the classics. An intense actress, she is also a comedienne. Edwige Feuillère made her name in 1937 in Becque's *La Parisienne* and in *La Dame aux Camellias*. She created roles in Cocteau's *L'Aigle à deux têtes* (The Eagle Has Two Heads) and Claudel's *Partage de Midi* (Spoils of Noon). Jean Cocteau (1889–1963) was a great theatrical showman, as well as being a novelist, film-maker and poet. His plays were concerned with love and death and include *La Voix humaine* (The Human Voice), a powerful monodrama, The Eagle Has Two Heads and *La Machine Infernale* (The Infernal Machine), based on the legend of Oedipus.

Most of Henri de Montherlant's plays were written between 1942 and 1954, with themes of church versus state, violence and nobility. *The Master of Santiago* and *Malatesta* are two of the best known.

An actor who died young was Gérard Phillipe (1922–59) a popular film star. He first made his name playing the title role in Camus's powerful *Caligula*.

The most remarkable partnership, professional and matrimonial, in the French theatre is that of Jean-Louis Barrault and Madeline Renaud. She made her debut at the Comédie-Française in 1925, marrying Barrault in 1940. He was at the great theatre from 1940–45, directing and acting, then the pair left to found the Compagnie Renaud-Barrault, a most adventurous and excellent organization, performing Duras, Montherlant, Camus etc. Renaud is a tragedienne but she is even better known for her stylish high comedy. Millions must know her husband's powers of mime from *Les*

Left: Charles Laughton's later film career does little to indicate what a fine actor he could be. Here he is playing the title role in Brecht's Galileo, *as performed in Washington and New York in 1947.*

Enfants du Paradis. He is total theatre in one person. He startled the Comédie-Française by his speed of delivery and by extending its repertoire, then triumphed at home and abroad with his new company. He is a famous Hamlet. In 1959 he became Director of the Theatre de France, the nation's second theatre, but was told to leave because he sympathized with the student-rioters of May 1968. Shortly before he had sponsored Roger Blin's important production of Genet's *Les Paravents* (The Stalking Horses). He now moved to an indoor wrestling stadium, converting it into a successful theatre where he directed, among other works, dramatizations of Rabelais. Europe and America welcomed his company. In 1972 a disused hall in a railway station was taken over, where he presented Claudel. When the authorities turned the building into a museum, he, his wife and his troupe, like earlier French companies, were on the move again, this time to the Palais de Glaces, an old ice rink. A new auditorium that sat 920 people was erected, plus a smaller one. The ghosts of Molière, Shakespeare and many other immortals must surely rejoice in their art, their courage and their stamina.

The Theatre of the Absurd is a term coined by the critic Martin Esslin in 1961. Man's absurd and purposeless existence has long been explored, but after Camus's *The Myth of Sisyphus* (1942) a number of dramatists wrote plays that could be grouped as a School of the Absurd: Samuel Beckett, Jean Genet, Max Frisch, Harold Pinter, Eugene Ionesco, N. F. Simpson, Edward Albee and others, though not *all* their plays. Beckett's *Waiting for Godot* (1953) is the first supreme example of the genre.

Born in Ireland in 1906, Beckett settled in France in 1937, and his most famous plays were written in French. *Godot* is a tragi-farce with two tramps waiting for the mysterious Mr. Godot, who may or may not be God. It comments on Man in our time, stranded in what appears a meaningless universe. *Endgame* has a pitiful group living in dustbins in a tower cut off from the world; *Krapp's Last Tape*, a character listening to an old tape-recording of his life. *Happy Days* has three characters and is acted twice. Other plays included *Play* and *Not I.*

Jean Genet, born in 1910, was a professional criminal who turned to drama. His world is one of rituals and dreams and fantasies of vice and violence,

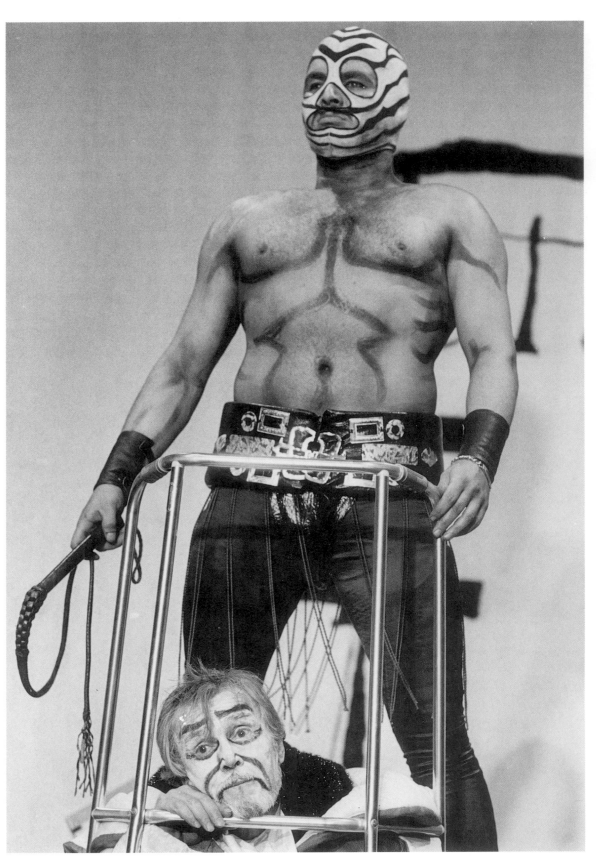

Right: Hugh Keays Byrne as the Executioner and Clement McCallin as the Judge in the Royal Shakespeare Company's production of Genet's The Balcony *in 1972.*

power and revenge. *The Maids* has despised servants turning to murder, *The Balcony* is set in a brothel. Other plays include *The Blacks* and *The Screens*, about Algerian peasants.

Romanian-born Eugène Ionesco is a notable and very influential French Absurdist, making his name with the uproarious *La Cantatrice chauve* (The Bald Prima Donna). In *Rhinocéros* all the townspeople turn into these aggressive beasts except Berenger, the moral being

the dangers of conformity. Other plays include *La Léçon, Les Chaises* and *Macbett* (The Lesson, The Chairs and Macbeth).

The Theatre of Cruelty was created by Antonin Artaud (1896–1948). He believed that it would banish the audience's violent and disorderly repressions by total theatre: music, frenzy, ritual, cruelty etc. True or not, it can make for exciting theatre, most notably Peter Brook's production of Peter Weiss's *Marat-Sade* in 1964.

LOOK FORWARD IN HOPE

Britain

The West End was much the same in the mid-1950s as it had been since the 1930s, as were the repertory companies, which were still unsubsidized. The author recalls reading about what was to happen at the Royal Court under its new management, the English Stage Company, just before setting off for a summer season at Cromer, the plays to be performed including *Bell, Book and Candle, Hippo Dances, The Moon is Blue, The Shadow of Doubt* etc., all sound West End/Broadway fare. What was said in advance about *Look Back in Anger* merely suggested that an old drama school friend, Kenneth Haigh, had landed a very good part and was well cast for it . . .

The English Stage Company had been founded by George Devine in 1955. He was one of the great Gielgud company at the Queen's Theatre before the war and director of the Old Vic School after it, also regularly directing at (what was then) the Shakespeare Memorial Theatre at Stratford-upon-Avon. He also directed a number of operas, greatly helping young singers to act, notably at Sadler's Wells. He had also played a notable Tesman to Peggy Ashcroft's Hedda Gabler in 1954; but above all he wanted to create a writer's theatre. He believed that the theatre is a temple of ideas, ideas expressed so well that it may be called art. He wanted the theatre to express an attitude and express it by fine writing. So, of course, have many others, but Devine, his assistant, Tony Richardson, and their colleagues achieved the temple of ideas. The company staged 450 plays in its first quarter of a century, many of them new. Devine died in 1966.

He and his colleagues gave writers the opportunity to set off the greatest explosion of native drama since the Elizabethans and Jacobeans, an upsurge of creative power that continues. The results were and are seen far beyond the small Royal Court Theatre in London.

The company's very first production was *The Mulberry Bush* by Angus Wilson in April 1956. Meanwhile, 750 new plays had poured into George Devine's office, one of them from a young actor, John Osborne, born in 1929, and destined to save 'the English theatre from death through gentility', as Angus Wilson the novelist put it.

Was it quite so genteel in 1956? Samuel Beckett had laid the foundations of the Theatre of the Absurd with his *Waiting for Godot* in 1953. It exasperated some, rather than shocking, though it was hailed by others. The Swiss dramatist Hochwälder was admired for his *The Strong are Lonely*, in which those unshrinking violets Donald Wolfit and Ernest Milton inspired Tynan to write: 'I shall long recall these two expert players stealthily upstaging each other for the greater glory of God.'

Ugo Betti, an Italian succesor to Pirandello, had died in 1953, and was now rewarded with no fewer than three plays in London, the best known of which was *The Queen and the Rebels*. Brecht's *The Threepenny Opera* had been successfully revived, and Ionesco's one-act *The Lesson* had crept into the Arts Theatre. Other West End fare, much of it excellent entertainment, included Feydeau's fizzing *Hotel Paradiso*; Anouilh's *The Waltz of the Toreadors*, directed by Peter Hall and with bravura performances by Hugh Griffith and Beatrix Lehmann; *The Rainmaker, Gigi* and other enjoyable shows. Gielgud and Ashcroft from Stratford led the company in *King Lear* and *Much Ado*,

Right: John Osborne, playwright, actor and history-maker.

while at the Phoenix were the combined talents of Peter Brook and Paul Scofield in *Hamlet*, *The Family Reunion* and Graham Greene's *The Power and The Glory*. Rattigan, Priestley and others were represented, as well as Peter Ustinov in his best play, *Romanov and Juliet*. By any standards this is a fine list, but of new British drama, of youthful drama, there is precious little. Worse, the valiant clubs could no longer keep going, the Arts apart. Grants for the theatre – even allowing that costs were not so high – were in their infancy still.

The breakthrough

Then came the breakthrough on 8 May 1956 with the first night of John Osborne's *Look Back in Anger*, even if few realized it. Legend has it that the reviews were scathing, but in fact only *The Times* had very little to say in its favour among the serious London papers. *The Birmingham Post* on evidence of the play decided that the venture must surely sink. However, on Sunday the situation was transformed by a good review in *The Sunday Times* by Harold Hobson and a famous one by Kenneth Tynan in *The Observer*, who agreed that the play would remain a minority taste, but thought it was roughly '6,733,000, the number of people in the country between twenty and thirty'. Then he finished with his famous: 'I doubt if I could love anyone who did not wish to see *Look Back in Anger*. It is the best young play of the decade.'

Despite this, the play did not prosper greatly at first, even though it was revived and filmed, and became a financial as well as an artistic success. Kenneth Haigh made his name in the title role of the 'Angry Young Man', as a clever publicity man dubbed the anti-hero Jimmy Porter. As with many first plays, it was a very personal statement indeed, its abrasive anti-hero, brutally witty and eloquent, became a national figure to many who never saw the play. Suddenly, it seemed, there were playwrights in plenty. Osborne, though nothing equalled the publicity attached to his verbally lacerating hero, the redbrick university educated working class sweet-stall holder, created a sympathetic friend in Chris, also a likeable ex-Indian army father-in-law. Jimmy's worst tirades are against his wife and her unseen mother. The rest of the cast were Mary Ure as the wife, Alan Bates as Cliff, Helena Hughes as Helena, the actress who replaces the wife, and John Welsh as Colonel Redfern. The play reached New York the next year and was warmly welcomed. 'Angry Young Men', became a tag for a whole movement of anti-establishment young writers.

Below: Feydeau's farce Hotel Paradiso, *staged in London in 1956 with Alec Guinness in the lead.*

Osborne followed this with the earlier written *Epitaph for George Dillon*, then *The Entertainer*, with its marvellous central role of Archie Rice, the third-rate music-hall comic, gloriously played by Laurence Olivier, with a running theme of England in decay. Like *Luther* and *Inadmissible Evidence* that followed in the early 1960s, it was a big success. *A Patriot for Me*, for some his finest play, is about an Austro-Hungarian officer who is blackmailed because of his homosexuality into becoming a spy, a story based on fact. There is a brilliant panoramic view of a period, complete with a famous transvestite ball scene. It was fortunate that the Royal Court was a club theatre or the censor would have struck. Later plays, *Time Present*, *A Hotel in Amsterdam* and the Pirandello-like *A Sense of Detachment*, have come under fire from those who resent growing objectivity, the disappearance of Jimmy Porter-like charactors, and an apparent move to the right. Yet they could not deny his theatrical flair, nor, as evinced in *West of Suez*, his feeling for the power and glory of the English language.

The same may be said of Harold Pinter. Born in 1930, and for some years a busy repertory actor, his first staged play was *The Birthday Party* in 1958. It was virtually destroyed without even a scandal by the critics with the exception of Harold Hobson in *The Sunday Times*, from the first a champion of the playwright. Though Pinter did not approve of the production, its total failure is still a puzzle, for it is as 'Pinteresque' as later plays, with the flair for prosaic, electric dialogue and the motives of key characters unrevealed. *The Room* written in 1957, and the even more menacing *The Dumb Waiter* were both produced in 1960, the year that others besides Hobson grasped that Pinter was a major playwright, for this was the year of *The Caretaker*, still his most famous play. It boasts two especially memorable characters, Ashton who has had electric shock treatment (when it was more primitive than it is now), played by Peter Woodthorpe, and Davies, the tramp, the third part in the famous cast being taken by Alan Bates.

Other fine plays include *The Homecoming*, which was Pinter's biggest Broadway success; *The Collector*, a comedy of manners; and the one-act *Silence*, part of a double bill staged by the Royal Shakespeare Company. The two parts were played by David Waller and Peggy Ashcroft, a husband and wife reminiscing, but not with each other. It has one of the most moving last lines in drama, which cannot be quoted out of context. Later plays include *No Man's Land* and *Betrayal*.

Pinter has had many successes as a director, screenplay writer and radio playwright, and was an associate director of the National Theatre. His influence on modern drama has been considerable, indeed imitators appeared, known as 'Pinteretti'. He has also given his name to the Pinter Pause. It is a far cry from that disastrous and only week of *The Birthday Party*.

Below: Kenneth Haigh and Mary Ure in Look Back in Anger *at the Royal Court, 1956.*

Left: Nicol Williamson in the leading role of John Osborne's Inadmissible Evidence, *one of the most testing parts in modern drama.*

Below: John Osborne's A Patriot for Me (1965) was revived at the Haymarket with Alan Bates as the Austro-Hungarian officer turned spy and Michael Gough as the drag queen in the 1983 production.

Above: Paul Scofield and Judy Parfitt, with David Burke behind them, in Osborne's A Hotel in Amsterdam.

Pinter's first wife, Vivien Merchant, was an ideal interpreter of his early plays and a remarkable actress in the classics. Her moving Bertha in James Joyce's *Exiles* at the Mermaid in 1970 and the Aldwych the next year was widely acclaimed.

On the strength of his *Sergeant Musgrave's Dance*, John Arden, born in 1930, seemed about to climb a pinnacle of dramatic fame and ability at least the equal of that of Osborne and Pinter. Set in Victorian England this 'historical parable' allowed modern comparisons to be made with military events in Cyprus in the last days of British rule. Musgrave and three companions come to a mining town, officially as a recruiting party, actually as deserters. Horrified by a reprisal he has committed, Musgrave determines to ram home his own experience of the horrors of war by an atrocity of his own. Despite his clear

hatred of violence, Arden does not load the dice too strongly on one side. He created an almost Brueghel-like world of reality, using Brechtian methods, including song and dance. Yet unlike Brecht and his more fervent disciples Arden recognizes the complexity of man and his environment.

Other plays include *Live Like Pigs*, *The Happy Haven*, *The Workhouse Donkey*, about corruption and power in a northern town, and *Armstrong's Last Goodnight*, with a fine performance by Albert Finney and invented dialect for this part border ballad. With his wife Margaretta D'Arcy he wrote *The Hero Rises Up* about Nelson, then came the notorious *The Island of the Mighty* in 1968. This resulted with their falling out with the producer, Trevor Nunn, whose production they publicly disowned. They picketed the Aldwych and there was a

famous scene when the audience shouted at John Arden to leave the stage so that the play could continue.

Robert Bolt, born in 1924, had a tremendous success with a play about a salesman, *Flowering Cherry*, starring Ralph Richardson and Celia Johnson. There followed his hugely popular *A Man for all Seasons*, starring Paul Scofield and Wendy Hiller, later turned into a memorable film. After this came *Vivat, Vivat Regina*, with Sarah Miles as Mary, Queen of Scots, and Eileen Atkins as Elizabeth I. The latter had been a fine Shakespearean since the early 1950s, also winning an award for her marvellous performance in Frank Marcus's gripping *The Killing of Sister George* in 1965 and New York in 1966. Her Elizabeth made her a star. It, too, was seen in New York.

Arnold Wesker, born in 1932, made his name with three plays about a Jewish family from 1936–59, *Chicken Soup with Barley, Roots* (1958), and *I'm Talking about Jerusalem* (1959). In fact, the family does not appear in his most famous play, which is *Roots*, in which Joan Plowright gave a notable performance. Later plays have included the scintillating *The Kitchen*, a day in the life of a restaurant's kitchen staff, which is also a view of the world. *Chips with Everything* is set on an R.A.F. station and creates a world in robot-like guise. It is both funny and powerful. Much of Wesker's time from 1962 was spent with Centre 42 which was created to bring art and drama to ordinary people with union backing. In 1972 the great music hall comedian Max Wall was very fine as Manny in another warm picture of Jewish life, *The Old Ones*, at the Royal Court.

Peter Shaffer, born in 1926, has had a number of successes, one of them

Above: Pinter's The Homecoming *with the playwright seated, Jane Lowe, Terence Rigby at the back and John Savident wielding a stick. A touring production at the Palace Theatre, Watford.*

Overleaf: John Arden's powerful Sergeant Musgrave's Dance *was revived at the Old Vic in 1984 with Albert Finney in the title role.*

Left: Dennis Quilley in drag in Privates on Parade by Peter Nichols, an exceptionally versatile performance in a powerfully entertaining play.

colossal. His twin Anthony wrote the dazzling thriller *Sleuth*, which at once mocked and revelled in the conventions of the detective genre. Anthony Quayle and Keith Baxter were the original stars in 1970. Peter Shaffer's first success was with *Five Finger Exercise* in 1958, a fine study of a tension-racked family. Other plays followed, then, in 1964, he created an epic, *The Royal Hunt of the Sun*, seen at the Chichester Festival, the National at the Old Vic and on Broadway. It brilliantly told the story of Pizarro's conquest of the Incas of Peru, with major performances from Colin Blakely as the Spanish leader and Robert Stephens as the Inca ruler Atahualpa, and with brilliant staging by John Dexter. Dexter was a key figure at the Royal Court before becoming an associate director of the National Theatre. From 1974–81 he was director of productions at the Metropolitan Opera, also staging Broadway plays.

Shaffer's most notable – its enemies would say notorious – play is *Amadeus*, about the hatred of the composer Salieri for the far more gifted, young and smutty-talking Mozart. It triumphed at the National with Scofield as Salieri, later at Her Majesty's with Frank Finlay and again on Broadway. Simon Callow was the first Mozart. It was later adapted to become an Oscar-winning film, all the versions being slightly different.

More Playwrights

Peter Nichols, born in 1927, writes plays more obviously biographical than most, comedy not deflecting the anguish in so many of them: *A Day in the Life of Joe Egg*, showing the effect on parents of a spastic child; *Forget-Me-Not Lane* with the author looking back at his adolescence; and, among others *Privates on Parade*. This is about a concert party of soldiers in Malaya in the 1950s. In it Dennis Quilley gave a legendary performance of theatrical 'camp' heading a marvel of a Royal Shakespeare Company cast. *Born in the Garden* gave Beryl Reid a wonderful role as an odd, recently widowed woman, while *Passion Play*, which caused some friction between Nichols and the Royal Shakespeare Company, was later put on by the author. It was a technical as well as a theatrical triumph. A tale of adultery is acted out by the two main characters, with their alter egos portrayed by two other actors, speaking their true thoughts. Playgoers benefit from the obvious fact that the playwright, as the poet Roger Woodis has noted, is 'a worried man, and that is his strength'.

Simon Gray, born in 1936, made his name with *Wise Child* (1967) and had a hit with *Butley* starring Alan Bates as a university lecturer whose life is collapsing about him. Gray also worked with Bates in *Stage Struck*, a fine comedy thriller (1979).

Opposite: Peter Shaffer's Equus *was first staged in 1973. The youth beside the towering 'horse' is David Dixon.*

Opposite: Beryl Reid and Peter Bowles in Peter Nichols's Born in the Garden.

Below: A Chorus of Disapproval by Alan Ayckbourn, staged at the National Theatre after starting life at the playwright's Scarborough theatre. Pictured are Michael Gambon (left) and Bob Peck.

In terms of productivity – let alone the pleasure he has given – Alan Ayckbourn, born in 1939, is a phenomenon. Not yet as prolific as de Vega, his output is prodigious, and is more remarkable still because he runs the Stephen Joseph Theatre-in-the-Round at Scarborough in Yorkshire, having become director of productions in 1970. Most of his plays begin their life there. Stephen Joseph, the son of the incomparable revue artist Hermione Gingold, was a brilliant teacher at the Central School of Speech and Drama and was already a believer in theatre-in-the-round. He died young in 1967, having failed to convert many to his belief, for the total round, as opposed to the three-quarters or even more, presents problems of communication that need no description. However, he toured the country with a portable theatre-in-the-round and founded the Victoria, Stoke-on-Trent, in 1962, having started his first such theatre in the public library at Scarborough seven years earlier. It was at Scarborough that Ayckbourn's first plays were staged, and, indeed, nearly all his plays since, though he first directed plays at the Victoria, Stoke-on-Trent. His first

London success was *Relatively Speaking.* His middle-class comedies and farcical comedies usually have some degree of despair in the background, sometimes in the foreground. He once had five running in London at one time, *Absurd Person Singular*, *Absent Friends* and his awe-inspiring trilogy, *The Norman Conquests* (1973). These recount the hilarious, awful events of a single weekend: the first play set in the dining room, the second in the sitting room and the third in the garden all giving different perspectives on the same people and happenings. All can be enjoyed separately or in any order, though there is an ideal one. The skill that this trilogy entailed is proof of craftsmanship of the highest order. Another of his plays, *Sisterly Feelings*, has four possible versions: which was played depended on the toss of a coin at the end of the first scene, and one of the actresses making a choice at the end of scene two. He is now famous in many parts of the world, and is often performed at the National Theatre, as befits a national phenomenon.

The most verbally dazzling of British leading playwrights is Tom Stoppard,

Right: Tom Stoppard's very successful Jumpers *at the National Theatre had a bravura performance by Michael Hordern.*

Opposite: Roger Rees and Felicity Kendal in Tom Stoppard's The Real Thing *at the Strand Theatre in 1982.*

who was born in Czechoslovakia in 1937. As well as his power to dazzle, he can intrigue, explode verbal fireworks, moralize fizzingly and speak up for freedom. He made his name with *Rosenkrantz and Guildenstern are Dead*, produced by the National Theatre in 1967. It will be recalled that they are Hamlet's friends, summoned to Elsinore by Claudius to spy on him, peripheral parts. Their actual scenes appear in Stoppard's play, but they are the leads, with Hamlet as a minor character. The puzzled pair and the play triumphed, also in New York.

Enter a Free Man came next, first seen in Hamburg, then going to London. There

followed *The Real Inspector Hound*, in which a pair of dramatic critics get dragged into the action of a play. After two more one-acters came the sparkling *Jumpers* at the National Theatre in 1972. Its Professor of Moral Philosophy was played with bravura by Michael Hordern, with Diana Rigg as his ex-showbusiness wife. The critic John Barber called it a 'stark raving sane play'. It is set in a crazy future, complete, indeed with gymnasts, and is an hilarious tribute to irrationality.

Meanwhile, the Royal Shakespeare Company was presenting his *Travesties*, with a debate raging on art in which Lenin and James Joyce were involved. Stoppard's English was now more

amazingly dextrous than ever. There
followed a double bill at the Arts, *Dirty
Linen* and *New-Found Land*, which ran for
four years, also *Every Good Boy Deserves
A Favour*, which featured a symphony
orchestra; then *Night and Day*, which
defends press freedom. His considerable
output includes a translation of
Schnitzler's *Das Weite Land* as *Undis-
covered Country* and Nestroy's *Einen Jux
will er sich machen* as *On The Razzle*, both
being given by the National Theatre. He
had a major West End success with *The
Real Thing*, starring Tom Conti and
Felicity Kendal.

The Royal Court Theatre

William Gaskill had worked at the Royal
Court Theatre since 1958, when he
directed a double bill of N. F. Simpson's
plays *A Resounding Tinkle* and *The Hole*,
both entertaining plays of the Absurd. He
directed widely afterwards including the
now legendary *The Recruiting Officer* at
the National in 1963, with Robert
Stephens superb as Plume. On Devine's
death Gaskill took over the Royal Court
until 1972, and it was run by Oscar
Lewenstein from 1972–77. The present
director, Max Stafford-Clark took over
in 1979.

David Storey, born in 1933, and the
author of the novel *This Sporting Life*,
proved a wide-ranging playwright fasci-
nated by detail, whose plays include *The
Changing Room*, *In Celebration* and the
impressionistic *Home* (1970). This gave
magnificent parts, magnificently played,
to Gielgud and Richardson as inmates of a

*Right: Edward Bond's
remarkable* Saved *at the
Royal Court in 1965. The
stoning scene caused a stir
that obscured the play's
merits.*

mental home. Charles Wood's plays were also staged, notably his *Veterans* (1972) starring Gielgud and John Mills. It was set on the location in Turkey for filming *The Charge of the Light Brigade*, on which Wood had worked as a script writer. His *'H'* was about General Havelock's march to Lucknow in the Indian Mutiny and the savage reprisals taken by the British. *Dingo* and *Jingo* are among his other plays, the first set in North Africa in a prisoner-of-war camp, the second a scathing attack on British complacency before the fall of Singapore in 1941. It was staged by the Royal Shakespeare Company. Wood was a regular for 15 years and his writing about the military has a conviction that most military plays lack.

It was in 1965 that Edward Bond, born in 1935, caused his first sensation. His *The Pope's Wedding* had had a 'production without decor' in 1962. Then came *Saved*, which includes a notorious scene where a baby is stoned to death, which caused an uproar and a criminal charge.

Bond is more highly regarded abroad than at home, but there is no doubting the power of his writing. His *Lear* was so savage that some felt it counter-productive, and his *Bingo* has Shakespeare being berated by Bond for not being more politically aware, a fascinating play. Bond has written two anti-apartheid plays, *Black Mass* and *Passion*, also *The Fool* and, in 1978, *The Woman*, the first new play to be staged in the Olivier Theatre at the National. It stems from Greek tragedy. His bleak vision of the world added to his powerful pen make him a constant challenge to audiences. There will never be anything bland about the writing of Edward Bond.

225

Right: Anthony Hopkins in Pravda *by David Hare and Howard Brenton, a tremendous performance in a powerful and entertaining play about Fleet Street.*

226

Howard Brenton, born in 1946, is a polemical political writer. Outraged by capitalism and its results, he is another writer who first got his chance at the Royal Court. Brenton's plays include *The Love of a Good Man* and *No End of Blame*. He and David Hare collaborated with great success in *Pravda* in 1985, which was staged at the Olivier Theatre, a splendid play casting a searing eye at newspaper moguls. It is a big bold play like its 'hero', Lambert Le Roux – who, inevitably, becomes a tremendous anti-hero, not quite the intention. Anthony Hopkins played the monster, according to an admiring Michael Billington, like a water buffalo with brains.

Brenton's early plays included *The Churchill Play*, set in 1984, with trades unionists being badly treated by the military. One of his most admired plays is *Weapons of Happiness*, the first première staged by the National in its new home on the South Bank. Howard Barker, master of dialogue and hater of capitalism, is another major talent.

David Hare's first success was *Slag* in 1971, set in a girl's school. Others include *The Great Exhibition*, written with Howard Brenton, which concerns three generations of Midlanders who are corrupt politically and personally. *Plenty* is about a woman striving to recapture the idealism she experienced in the Second World War.

The South African playwright Athol Fugard, born in 1932, uses drama to strike at apartheid in human terms. That he is a very fine playwright makes his voice even more powerful. He has been writing plays since the 1950s.

His first major success was *The Blood Knot*, seen in London in 1963, and New York in 1964, with the great James Earl Jones in the leading role. The play has a searing theme, the temptation to pretend to be white in a society split by segregation. He and his actress wife Sheila Meiring set up an amateur drama group in New Brighton, Port Elizabeth, in 1963, which has ranged from Sophocles and Brecht to his own plays. This is very much a group theatre and from it have stemmed a number of important plays stressing the point of view of black South Africa. They include *Sizwe Bansi Is Dead*, about the harsh pass laws, and *The Island*, where two prisoners are confined. Both plays were later staged in New York, with John Kani and Winston Ntshona as actors and co-authors. *Dimetos* was commissioned by the Edinburgh Festival in 1975; Paul

Below: Athol Fugard's Master Harold and the Boys, *staged at the National Theatre in 1983 with, left to right, Ramolao Makhene, Duart Slywain and John Kani.*

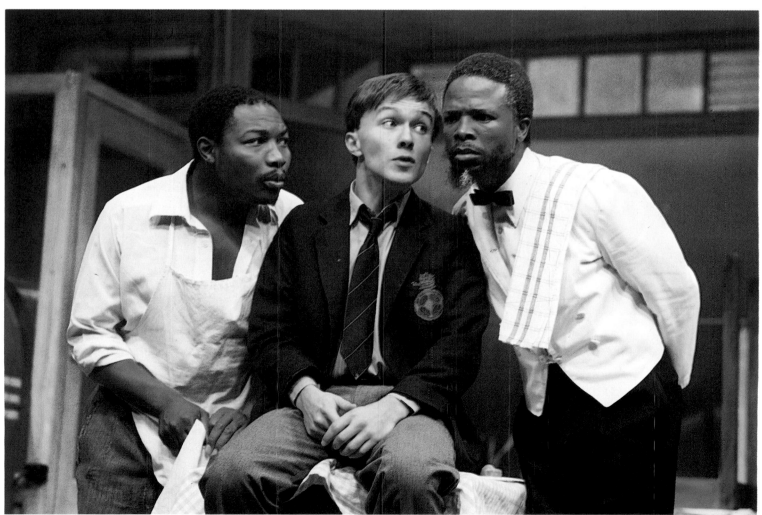

Scofield later played the lead in it in a Nottingham Playhouse production that went to London, while *A Lesson from Aloes* was staged at the National Theatre's Cottesloe in London in 1980 and in New York with James Earl Jones. Recent plays include *The Road to Mecca*, staged by Yale Repertory Theatre in 1983 and the National Theatre in 1985.

The West End did not feel threatened by events at the Royal Court, indeed some plays, mostly a number of John Osborne's, were transferred. Newspapers made much of the alleged anti-establishment nature of the Royal Court, the theatre establishment included. This rang hollow when, as noted, Olivier joined the company to give a marvel of a performance as Archie Rice. Osborne was the first Englishman to write a great part for a great actor since the seventeenth century. Almost as remarkable a double was Nicol Williamson as Osborne's Maitland in *Inadmissible Evidence*.

The impact of *West Side Story* and *My Fair Lady* has been noted. The only British musical in fairly traditional form was Lionel Bart's one great success, *Oliver* (1960), based on *Oliver Twist*. Book, lyrics and music – it was a riot of good tunes – added up to a near flawless show, close to folk opera with a famous design by Sean Kenney, a very gifted designer who died in his early forties in 1973. Ron Moody was the splendid Fagin.

The finest musical of the period – using the term widely – was Joan Littlewood's *Oh, What A Lovely War!* in 1963. She had founded the Theatre Workshop in Manchester, but took over the Theatre Royal, Stratford East in London, in 1953 after touring the north of England with plays by Ewan McCall and some classics. Littlewood presented stunning shows that were influenced by Brecht, social concern, music hall, song and dance. She was very much the co-author of most shows. Only her classic productions were somewhat unconvincing. Brendan Behan's *The Quare Fellow* and *The Hostage* had enormous impact, and Shelagh Delaney's *A Taste of Honey* was a great success, but her fame rests above all on *Oh, What A Lovely War!*, an inspirational

Right: Leonard Rossiter's last role was the lead in Joe Orton's Loot. He died during a performance. Gemma Craven is with him.

Left: Peggy Ashcroft as
Queen Margaret and
Donald Sinden as York in
Henry VI, part of the
Wars of the Roses cycle at
Stratford directed by Peter
Hall and designed by John
Bury, 1963–64.

production with the famous old songs of
the First World War turning the music
hall-cum-dramatic style of the show into a
harrowingly emotive whole. It later had a
long West End run. It was a great success
in many countries. It was finely filmed,
but it belongs to the stage. Alas for
Britain, Joan Littlewood, having lost
many of her group because of their
success, became a comet-like roamer, in
Europe, Africa, America and elsewhere.

Three farces deserve a mention: the
first the traditional *Sailor Beware!* by
Philip King of *See How They Run* fame.
Opening in 1955, it made a star of Peggy
Mount as Emma Hornett, a stereotyped
mother-in-law-to-be. The surge and
thunder of Miss Mount was the delight of
everyone who saw her – and the despair of
rep actresses trying in a week or two to
equal her atomic power.

There was also the appearance of
Henry Livings, expert in farce and
comedy, whose *Stop It, Whoever You Are*,
its hero a lavatory attendant called Perkin
Warbeck, proclaimed that a new and
major comic talent had arrived. Wilfred
Brambell was Perkin. And there was Joe
Orton, master of black farce, whose *Loot*,
especially, first staged by Charles
Marowitz, made his name. He died
young.

The Royal Shakespeare Company

By the end of the 1950s subsidies for the
arts, without being as generous as those in
many other European countries, were a
part of serious theatre life. It was just as
well, as the classics were too expensive to
stage, especially Shakespeare with his
large casts, without subsidy. The
Shakespeare Memorial Theatre at

Stratford-upon-Avon, under Anthony Quayle and Gen Byam Shaw, had risen to new heights. History was made when Olivier played Macbeth, directed by Byam Shaw and – in a very famous production by Peter Brook, Titus Andronicus. *Coriolanus*, directed by Peter Hall in 1959, gave Olivier another triumph, but the theatre by this time needed a single, very strong hand to guide it.

Peter Hall, best known for his work at the Arts Theatre in the mid-1950s, when he directed *Waiting for Godot*, Anouilh's *Waltz of the Toreadors* and *Mourning Becomes Electra*, became director of what was renamed the Royal Shakespeare Company in 1960, and in the same year the company established a London base at the Aldwych Theatre, despite hostility from West End theatre managers.

A born administrator as well as a major director, Hall inherited a well-run successful theatre and boldly transformed it into an even greater institution. Long-term contracts for members of the company – with chances to leave and do other, often more lucrative, work – made for a strong and confident ensemble. Modern plays were staged at the Aldwych, along with Shakespeare transfers from Stratford and other classics and Hall chose two major talents to work with him, Michel St. Denis and Peter Brook. But it was Hall's theatre, not least because of his flair as a businessman as well as an artist.

The first contract artists included Peggy Ashcroft, Richard Johnson, Eric Porter, Dorothy Tutin, Ian Bannen and Peter O'Toole. John Barton was a key figure – as a Shakespearean scholar as well as a major director: *Twelfth Night* and *Troilus and Cressida* were among his great successes, also, as co-director, *The Wars of the Roses* (1963), the three *Henry VI* plays and *Richard III*. These all established the new ensemble, which included Peggy Ashcroft as Queen Margaret, Donald Sinden as York, David Warner as Henry VI and Ian Holm as Richard III. Early modern triumphs included Peter Weiss's *Marat-Sade* with Ian Richardson as Marat, Glenda Jackson as Charlotte Corday and Patrick Magee as de Sade, directed by Peter Brook. The play was inspired by the French director, Antonin Artaud, of Theatre of Cruelty fame. The audience, suffering with the actors, has its repressions released.

Right: Peter Brook put A Midsummer Night's Dream *into a circus/gymnasium setting for his 1970 production by the Royal Shakespeare Company and had an historic triumph. Alan Howard (left) and John Kane are the actors playing Theseus and Puck.*

Trevor Nunn took over from Peter Hall in 1968. He created Stratford's Other Place, opened the Warehouse in London, and has directed a wealth of plays, including an outstanding *Macbeth* at the Other Place in 1976. Alan Howard's achievements with the company have been particularly notable, including his Henry VI, Coriolanus, Hamlet and Henry V, the Henrys as part of a magnificent *Wars of the Roses* cycle directed by Terry Hands. *Nicholas Nickleby* in 1980 was a national glory and is now being revived. Also famous was Peter Brook's *A Midsummer Night's Dream* in 1970 at a moment when the company's financial state was dire. It was the most acclaimed staging of any Shakespearean comedy in memory, a magical conjuring up of the circus and *commedia dell'arte*, yet the verse seemed clearer than ever before. It was seen in Stratford, London, Europe and North America.

Now the company has its new and second home in the Barbican Centre in the City of London, opened in 1982 with *Henry IV*, Joss Ackland as a superb Falstaff. Its members may become stars

233

elsewhere – Ben Kingsley, one of a number – but the Royal Shakespeare Company, also blessed by the incomparable voice coach Cis Berry, remains home for many of the actors.

The National Theatre

A National Theatre had been a dream since the eighteenth century. Finally the foundation stone was laid on the south bank of the Thames in 1951 and building began late in 1969.

By this time the National Theatre as a company had been flourishing mightily at the Old Vic, Lilian Baylis's beloved theatre.

It was decided in 1962 that the Old Vic should at first house the National, which meant the end of the Old Vic Company. Its last performance was given in June 1963. The National Theatre Company was based on the company of the Chichester Festival Theatre, which opened in July 1962, inspired by Stratford, Ontario's Festival Theatre. The local hero at Chichester was Leslie Evershed-Martin.

The opening night of the National Theatre in October 1963 featured *Hamlet*, with the prince played by Peter O'Toole, who had earlier made his name at the Bristol Old Vic. He is notably good

Right: Olivier as Othello, 1964.

236

in Shaw. A fine Shylock at Stratford, and a decent Hamlet, his later Macbeth at the Old Vic was, like the evening, so disastrous that it more than lived up to the Curse of Macbeth tradition.

Chichester had a fine company, whose high spot was *Uncle Vanya* in 1963 with Michael Redgrave in the title role, Olivier as Astrov, Joan Plowright as Sonya, and Rosemary Harris as Ilyena. John Clements took over from Olivier in 1966, and famous performances in his day included Alastair Sim in *The Magistrate* and Maggie Smith in *The Country Wife*. Clements's long and distinguished career has included a production of *The Beaux' Strategem* that opened at the Phoenix in 1949 starring himself and his wife Kay Hammond which ran for 532 performances, an astonishing feat for a classic revival.

At the National, Olivier had John Dexter and William Gaskill as his talented associate directors. Michael Blakemore became one in 1972 and Frank Dunlop founded the nearby Young Vic in 1970.

The National Theatre building, with three auditoria, the Olivier, Lyttleton and Cottesloe Theatres, opened in 1976. There have been too many magnificent National Theatre productions, at the Old Vic and on the South Bank, to attempt to

record them here. Some have been mentioned earlier, others that are recalled, personally and with joy, were Zeffirelli's *Much Ado*; Miller's *The Merchant of Venice* with Olivier, and his *The School for Scandal*; Michael Blakemore's production of *The Front Page*; Eduardo de Fillipo's *Saturday Sunday Monday*; and Arthur Miller's *Death of a Salesman*, directed by Michael Rudman, with Warren Mitchell as Willy Loman. Also to be saluted is the hugely successful restoration of Mystery Plays to the repertoire, the especial triumph of Bill Bryden.

At the time of writing in early 1986, one can look back at the National Theatre, financially under stress, taking Hall's production of *Coriolanus*, with Ian McKellen so fine in the title role, to Greece, birthplace of European drama. To his Chekhov performances he also added Sheridan's Mr Puff in *The Critic*. Anthony Sher's Richard III reached the Barbican from Stratford, proving the finest Demon King since Olivier, while at Stratford Kenneth Branagh achieved a triumph as Henry V, again never easy in the mighty shadow of Olivier, the first actor to become a life peer.

Above: Franco Zeffirelli's stunning Much Ado About Nothing *for the National Theatre at the Old Vic in 1965, with Maggie Smith and Robert Stephens as Beatrice and Benedick.*

237

In the West End one must applaud Ray Cooney and other experienced masters of farce, writers as well as actors, who established the Theatre of Comedy, presenting new, and old comedies, farcical comedies and farces with expert casts at more than one theatre. Michael Frayn's *Noises Off* is not one of them, but, apart from its being very funny, must be mentioned for having perhaps the most difficult single act to perform ever written, a backstage view of a disastrous play when everything is going wrong on stage and behind the scenes. The director of the London production was Michael Blakemore. Nicky Henson and his successors perform prodigies of comic athleticism.

Musicals of every sort abound and pay despite the grim cost of staging them: Andrew Lloyd Webber's *Cats* directed by Trevor Nunn; *Barnum*, with an agile Michael Crawford; *Les Misérables*, the RSC's action-packed musical of Victor Hugo's novel; the superb *Guys and Dolls* from the National; and others including *Me and My Girl* from the 1930s. Frank Finlay, one of the National's finest actors, appeared with David Essex as his Fletcher Christian in *Mutiny!* Will *Macbeth*,

already an opera, soon be a musical?

The situation elsewhere in Britain at the time of writing is variable and hard to assess, mainly because of costs, of financial cutbacks which, if implemented, may not close theatres, but can devastate standards. It matters that major and merely good and decent companies survive, that the famous Bristol Old Vic, where so many of today's leading actors have appeared, can be financially embarrassed, though keeping up the highest standards. It matters that good and decent companies survive, companies like the famous Glasgow Citizens, founded in 1943 by James Bridie, author of *Mr Bolfry* and *A Sleeping Clergyman*, and Paul Vincent Carrol, himself a noted Irish dramatist and the author of *Shadow and Substance*. Glasgow, even more than Edinburgh, is the cultural capital of Scotland, being also the home of Scottish Opera. It matters that Bath's historic Theatre Royal thrives, also the Crucible at Sheffield, the Haymarket Studio in Leicester, Opera North, based in Leeds. And the Royal Exchange at Manchester, like the Halle Orchestra, is more than a regional organization.

Right: Michael Frayn's dazzling farce Noises Off, with its second cast. Left to right, Robert Flemyng, Gabrielle Drake, Mandy Perryment, Glyn Grain, John Quayle and Phillida Law. They are being viewed by the play-within-a-play's director, the unseen Benjamin Whitrow.

Below: Andrew Lloyd Webber's Evita, one of his fabulously successful musicals, which was about the Peróns, played by Joss Ackland and Elaine Page.

242

Australia

The first recorded theatrical performance in Australia was at Sydney in 1789, Farquhar's *The Recruiting Officer*. Not until after the Second World War did a true school of native drama develop, helped by the success overseas of Ray Lawler's *The Summer of the Seventeenth Doll*, first staged by the new Elizabethan Theatre Trust in Melbourne in 1956. Partly thanks to the great Australian opera singer Nellie Melba, opera has had a good following in Australia, helped later by Joan Sutherland and her husband Richard Bonynge – and the Sydney Opera House. Now drama has come into its own, other playwrights of note including Richard Benyon, Alan Seymour, Patrick White, Peter Kenna, Hal Porter and Alan Hopgood. Australian actors are more likely to stay at home now because of tighter British immigration laws, which at least therefore have one benefit.

John McCullum, a popular film actor, has done much for drama in Australia, along with his wife, Googie Withers. He has been a manager and director, and his own play, *As It's Played Today*, is a fine one.

New Zealand

The best-known theatre figure in New Zealand has been Ngaio Marsh, the brilliant thriller writer, who did much valiant work for the stage. It has been an uphill battle, not least to keep local talent at home. Subsidies began in 1964 with the founding of the Queen Elizabeth II Arts Council. One of the nation's most successful playwrights is Roger Hall, whose *Middle Age Spread* had a good run at the Lyric in London in 1977.

Below: Two leading ladies of crime, Agatha Christie (left) and Ngaio Marsh, the latter doing much good for the theatre in her native New Zealand.

America

In the 1960s the future of the American theatre looked bleak, notably on Broadway, but regional theatres were beginning to open. Margo Jones had the first theatre-in-the-round in Dallas, Texas in 1945. It was the precursor of other groups, including Zelda Fichandler's Arena Stage in Washington D.C., which opened with *She Stoops To Conquer* and still flourishes, presenting American and European plays.

Broadway, meanwhile, was deep in trouble, although a strike by actors had one good effect: cheap previews instead of expensive out-of-town openings. In 1967 the Theater Development fund began valuable operations, subsidizing good plays with public and private money and providing tickets at reduced prices.

In 1962 Edward Albee, born in 1928, had a major success with *Who's Afraid of Virginia Woolf*, which was later filmed. He had earlier made his name with *Zoo Story* and *The American Dream*, which showed him to be in the leading line of American dramatists. However his other plays including *Tiny Alice, A Delicate Balance* and *Seascape* have not quite lived up to his promise. His is a despairing voice, which has perhaps affected his popularity.

More and more British plays have crossed the Atlantic, not least because of the enormous expense of staging shows on Broadway. Pinter, Bolt and Stoppard, as well as Osborne, were among the newcomers to America in the 1950s and 1960s.

The most successful Broadway playwright since the early 1960s has been Neil Simon, whose first success was *Come Blow Your Horn*. The films of his plays have been successful in Britain, but not the plays themselves, strangely. The leading avant-garde playwright is Sam Shepard, born in 1943, whose finest play is perhaps *Buried Child*, which won him a Pulitzer Prize. Also much admired is David Mamet, born in Chicago in 1947 and a co-founder of the St. Nicholas Theatre Company. His *American Buffalo*, about two small-time crooks attempting to steal a coin collection, was staged on Broadway and at the Cottesloe at the National Theatre in London. His *Glengarry Glen Ross* (1984) won a Pulitzer Prize. It originated in Chicago, as did Sam Shepard's *True West*. Other fine plays include a dazzling thriller, *Deathtrap*, by Ira Levin; Bernard Pomerance's *The*

Opposite: Edward Albee's Who's Afraid of Virginia Woolf? with Paul Eddington and Margaret Tyzack as the battling husband and wife and Mary Maddox and David Schofield (not pictured here) as their amazed visitors. It was directed at the National Theatre by Nancy Meckler.

245

Elephant Man; and Jack Gelber's *The Connection,* about drug addicts, which was given in London in 1961. He also directed Arthur Kopit's *Indians* for the Royal Shakespeare Company. Robert Anderson, author of the well-known *Tea and Sympathy,* is a considerable explorer of human relationships. His four plays that comprise *You Know I Can't Hear You When the Water's Running* were seen on both sides of the Atlantic in the 1960s. Pomerance's masterpiece *Melons* has only been seen in London.

The most extraordinary figure in current American theatre, a veritable combination of Lilian Baylis and Tyrone Guthrie, is Joseph Papp. Born in 1921, and with credits that range from *Hair* to *Hamlet,* he started the New York Shakespeare Festival in 1954 in a church. He next used a portable stage in a park, then in 1957 the City gave him a site in Central Park. Other sites there followed until glory day came with the opening of the Delacorte in the park in 1962, a public and private enterprise. Famous names were attracted to work for him, including Julie Harris, Colleen Dewhurst and James Earl Jones, a most notable Shakespearian, classical and modern player, who won a Tony – the major annual theatrical award – for his performance as the boxer Jack Johnson in *The Great White Hope* in 1968.

Papp produced a very successful musical, *Two Gentlemen of Verona,* in 1971, then founded the Public Theater in 1967, opening it with *Hair.* Jason Miller's *That Championship Season* and *A Chorus Line* are just two of the shows that started there. New York has now given it a subsidy, an enlightened and happy sign.

Meanwhile Papp became director of the Vivien Beaumont and the Mitzi E. Newhouse Theaters in 1973, but a cash crisis ended his management of them. Worse was to come. In 1980 the Delacorte could stage only one show, a modern version of *The Pirates of Penzance*. It was a mighty only, for it was a huge success, moving to the Uris Theater for a long run and also conquered London. Then the City of New York gave him a permanent subsidy and Shakespeare was heard and seen in Central Park. At the time of writing Papp seems as powerful a figure as anyone in the Anglo-American theatre.

One of the many young actors to get a chance from Joseph Papp was Stacy Keach, born in 1941. He made his New York debut at the Delacorte playing Marcellus and the First Player in *Hamlet* in 1964. In 1972 he was hailed by theatre critic Clive Barnes as the finest American Hamlet since John Barrymore. Few leading American actors in their forties can have done so much classical work, and he is also a notable player of O'Neill in New York and London. At the Delacorte he has played Falstaff in both parts of *Henry IV*, and his Broadway successes include Buffalo Bill in *Indians*, noted above.

Below: Richard III *at New York's Delacorte in Central Park where Shakespeare is presented free.*

Mention must also be made of the emergence of Los Angeles as a great theatre city, complete with the Los Angeles Theater Center, master-minded by Bill Bushnell.

To end on a classical and modern note it seems apt to go to Minneapolis and its Guthrie Theater. It was Tyrone Guthrie's last creation, with Tanya Moiseiwitsch and, being in the right hands, it has the right to fail as well as succeed. It seats over 1,400 people, none more than 52 feet from the stage and was opened in 1963. The stage is a thrust one with seven sides. Zoe Caldwell, Jessica Tandy and Hume Cronyn were in the original company in 1963, which opened with a perfect quartet, *Hamlet*, *The Three Sisters*, *Death of a Salesman* and Molière's *The Miser*. Later directors have included Michael Langham, who had succeeded Guthrie at Stratford, Ontario, Alvin Epstein, and Liviu Ciulei. There is an eleven-month season during which nine plays are presented. Guthrie's legs, like Antony's, bestride the ocean. So do Shakespeare's.

What does the future hold for the theatre? There is no easy answer, for its importance in people's lives varies from nation to nation. Since the Second World War Britain has joined the rest of Europe in subsidizing the performing arts, without which help they would perish, so high are today's costs. Subsidies never seem enough, while, of course, they cannot ensure great art. Yet they allow it to survive and stimulate quality and greatness. The United States, and notably some cities, especially New York, have begun to realize the necessity of helping – saving — the live theatre, which also has generous patrons, but there is always the threat of cutbacks. Watchful optimism is perhaps the way to see the future. The English survived the total annihilation of their theatre – the finest ever known – and arguably have the finest once again, though it is now the British theatre. Who knows which nation may next produce a true giant, a successor to the arts' supreme genius.

Above: Joseph Papp's The Pirates of Penzance *helped the Delacorte out of a financial crisis, since when its future has been secured. The show triumphed at Drury Lane.*

BIBLIOGRAPHY

The author wishes especially to acknowledge two monumental works, *The Oxford Companion to the Theatre*, edited by Phyllis Hartnoll, and *The Reader's Encyclopedia of World Drama*, edited by John Gassner and Edward Quinn (Methuen 1970).

James Agate: *These Were Actors* (Hutchinson 1943)

Brooks Atkinson: *Broadway* (Cassell 1971)

Sally Beauman: *The Royal Shakespeare Company* (Oxford 1982)

Margot Berthold: *a History of World Theater* (Ungar 1972)

Michael Billington: *The Guinness Book of Theatre Facts and Feats* (Guinness Superlatives 1982), *The Modern Actor* (Hamish Hamilton 1973)

Ivor Brown: *Shakespeare* (Collins 1949)

Harold Clurman: *The Fervent Years* (Secker and Warburg 1957)

Bamber Gascoigne: *World Theatre* (Ebury Press 1968)

Moss Hart: *Act I* (Random House 1959)

Ronald Harwood: *Sir Donald Wolfit* (Secker and Warburg 1971)

Laurence Irving: *Henry Irving* (Faber and Faber 1951)

A. M. Nagler: *A Source Book in Theatrical History* (Dover 1952)

Constantin Stanislavski: *My Life in Art* (Eyre Methuen 1980)

Howard Taubman: *The Making of the American Theatre* (Longmans 1967)

John Russell Taylor: *Anger and After* (Pelican 1963), *A Dictionary of the Theatre* (Penguin 1966)

J. C. Trewin: *Peter Brook* (Macdonald 1971)

Kenneth Tynan: *Tynan Right and Left* (Longmans 1967)

Audrey Williamson: *Old Vic Drama* (Rockcliff 1948)

INDEX